W0115637

BEING BLACK IN CORPORATE AMERICA

OJ SMITH

Being Black in Corporate America

© 2020 by OJ Smith

All rights reserved. This book or any portion thereof may not be reproduced
or used in any manner whatsoever without the express written permission
of the publisher except for the use of brief quotations in a book review.

ISBN (Print): 978-1-09834-354-5
ISBN (eBook): 978-1-09834-355-2

"If there is no struggle, there is no progress…

This struggle may be a moral one; or it may be a physical one; or it may be both moral and physical; but it must be a struggle".

—Frederick Douglass

TABLE OF CONTENTS

ACKNOWLEDGEMENTS

Well here we are with book #3. As my mind churns, I write outlines for my books. This book was created many years ago when I worked in Corporate America. Originally, this was to be my fifth book but with all of the attention to the racial matters in our country and world today I thought it most appropriate to move this up in the order. Writing this book has been different from books 1 & 2 because it shows that some of the racial divide is still the same today as it was when this book was written.

As I've said before, when we get older, we may find ourselves sitting, thinking and reflecting on the past. Our past. I certainly do. Other times as we try to describe who we are or why we feel or react in certain ways it takes us back to moments or images that created those feelings. At least it does with me.

One thing is a constant, for sure, whether we know this or not;
GOD IS, HAS ALWAYS BEEN, AND WILL ALWAYS BE.

I dedicate this book to the families and supporters of Breonna Taylor, George Floyd, Trayvon Martin, Rayshard Brooks, Botham Jean, Rodney King, Reginald Denny and Emmett Till.

Thanks to all my beta readers.

Thanks Lisa for listening, for your feedback, love, support and 33 years and counting.

Thanks Gregg Mansell; you rock dude.

Thanks Brandon and Candace for your feedback. Daddy loves you.

Thanks Dwonna Lenoir, Debbie Young and Lynn DuBose. I really appreciate your sincere interest, time and honest feedback.

Thanks Tony, for keeping it real with me. For the countless hours of candid conversation and feedback and memory-sharing moments we've had on this project.

Thanks Momma and Nici for always being involved and supportive.

Thanks Lynn Dubose and Pages Book Club, your support to me as a writer has been unparalleled.

Thanks E for the solid feedback and the desire to help.

Thanks to Toy and Squeeta for your desire to read and share. Your time and willingness to share your thoughts and feedback was very helpful. I really absorbed everything you shared.

Thanks to my Sands Chris, for keeping it 100.

I really appreciated this part of the process.

Thanks to my publisher, copy editor, illustrator and graphic designer BookBaby for your expertise and time in polishing my manuscript.

Thanks Antwon for helping me design my logo, which has become my book cover.

Thanks to all of my personal mentors (My Dudes, My Boyz, My Brothers) who provided me the day-to-day support and encouragement to write. Will Big Dawg, Mac, Fred, Tree, Hodge, Billy, Squeeta, Eric, SJ, MRob,

B McKorkel, My Sands #8 Chris and #5 Chuck. All mighty men of God. We are "Blessed and Highly Favored."

Shout out to my biking crew #on your left. Toy, Cheree, Squeeta and E. All the miles we put in on those bike paths and conversations along the way really kept my writing wheels turning and inspired a lot of it.

I sincerely believe we are within our due season for God's supernatural, super-sized TODAY and NOW blessings.

Get Ready! Get Ready! Get Ready!

From this point on in this book all the names have been disguised to respect and protect the privacy of the actual characters."

BEING BLACK IN CORP AMERICA

I don't profess to be a "know it all" but I do believe I truly have an understanding on why so many companies miss the mark, and others hit the mark, when it comes to dealing with minorities in the workplace. In particular, Blacks in Corporate America companies. Fortune 500 companies. White and blue collar employers.

I actually believe this book can serve as a guide to help employers' better handle workforce relations with minorities (African Americans) and ultimately all employees.

Two books ago, I wrote *HEALTHY MARRIAGES,* 19 Principles Designed to Rejuvenate Your Marriage. Within the book I stated I don't believe in the "perfect marriage" but I do believe in healthy marriages. A perfect marriage suggests "perfection" nothing is ever wrong or out of alignment. Healthy Marriages make good out of tough situations. In a Healthy Marriage you deal with real life obstacles and manage to survive and even be drawn closer together as partners. In that book I talk about 3 concepts to begin your approach towards developing a healthy relationship. Self-Conviction, Repair and ABCnD's (communication). I'll refresh the meaning of the three shortly. Similarly, I don't believe in the perfect job. Even a dream job (NFL superstar, actor or actress) has its ups and downs.

In my 2nd book *The Reinvention of OJ Smith* (my autobiography), I clearly talk about the many obstacles I've overcome in life to get to where I am today. Similarly, I believe the same applies to the Corporate America workforce. In particular to the Black leaders in the corporate world.

Self-Conviction

When you self-convict, the first thing you want to do is stand in front of the mirror. It is almost impossible to lie to yourself when you look at your reflection. So when you're identifying where you have missed the mark in any of the principles, be sure you are looking at yourself in a mirror. In more contemporary terms, you messed up and you're acknowledging to yourself you did. I can't emphasize enough how much easier life is when you admit mistakes. The longer you blame someone, or something else, the longer a problematic situation will persist. So, own up.

Let's take what's happening in our country today. We've experienced the shooting of Breonna Taylor in her home. **Breonna Taylor**, 26, was an EMT and aspiring nurse who was shot to death by police in her own home on March 13, 2020. It was described as a "botched raid;" officers barged into Taylor's apartment in Louisville, Kentucky, as she lay sleeping, and fired multiple rounds. Taylor was shot eight times by the police. Her killing was the result of a botched drug-warrant execution. No drugs were found; the warrant in question targeted another person, who lived miles away and who was already at the time in police custody.

We've experienced the knee on the neck of George Floyd, which would eventually kill him. We've experienced the shooting of 17-year-old Trayvon Martin. We've experienced two shots in the back of Rayshard Brooks, which eventually killed him.

On the night of June 12, 2020, **Rayshard Brooks**, a 27-year-old African American man, was fatally shot by an Atlanta Police officer. Two police officers responded to a complaint that Brooks was asleep in a car blocking a restaurant drive-through lane.

The officers began to handcuff Brooks. Brooks scuffled with the officers, got hold of one of the officer's taser, punched the other officer, and ran. With the officer pursuing him, Brooks half-turned and fired the taser toward the police officer, who then shot Brooks twice from behind while a third shot struck an occupied car. Brooks died after surgery.

We've experienced the fatal shooting of unarmed Botham Jean.

Botham Jean was a 26-year-old accountant who in September 2018 was fatally shot by an off-duty Dallas police officer who entered his apartment thinking it was her own apartment and mistook Jean for a burglar.

We all experienced the brutal beatings of Rodney King and Reginald Denny. **Rodney King** was an American man who was a victim of brutality by the Los Angeles Police Department. On March 3, 1991, King was beaten by LAPD officers after a high-speed chase during his arrest for drunk driving. A civilian, George Holliday, filmed the incident from his nearby balcony and sent the footage to a local news station. The footage clearly showed an unarmed King on the ground being beaten after initially evading arrest. The incident was covered by news media around the world and caused a public furor.

Reginald Denny is the White former construction truck driver who was pulled from his truck and beaten during the 1992 Los Angeles riots by a group of Black men. The attack was captured on video and broadcast live on national television. Four other Black LA residents who had been witnessing the attack on live television came to the aid of Denny by getting him to a hospital. While their beatings weren't fatal they were extremely painful for me to watch. We've all experienced the brutal slaying of 14-year-old Emmett Till. **Emmett Till** was an African American who was lynched, severely beaten, mutilated, shot and thrown into Mississippi's Tallahatchie river in 1955 after being accused of offending a White woman in her family's grocery store. His killers were acquitted in my opinion primarily because there was not a court in Mississippi that would ever convict a White for killing a Black.

In my opinion, what these events have in common is they've all touched our racial emotions. As the country goes into a mode of such high racial sensitivity it can sometimes create feelings that are uncomfortable. We see it in reactions in schools, churches and even in the workplace. The problem is, when it's not appropriately addressed, there's opinionated gossiping that leads to misunderstandings and perhaps even argumentative altercations. You could be in church and the family sitting right next to you has a totally different perspective than you on the *Trayvon vs. Zimmerman* case. How awkward and uncomfortable it would be when the two families engage in conversation and find out you have opposite perspectives on this. Imagine two school classmates who share different perspectives on the George Floyd killing. Over lunch when the topic comes out neither can believe how they've been that person's friend for this long if they think like that. Then all of a sudden these two good friends are friends no more.

The other thing in common is that the perpetrators have never self-convicted. Remember, self-conviction is not an acknowledgement of guilt. It just says your actions could have possibly led to a different outcome. I'd like to think whenever someone is killed the human heart will always root a different outcome. They've all tried to justify why what they did was necessary. In some cases they've never even acknowledged wrongdoings. This even with the fact that in 1956, Till's killers publicly admitted they killed him. They knew they were protected against double jeopardy. The point I'm trying to make is if we never acknowledge or self convict, how can we ever move forward. Without self-conviction, the act or behavior will simply continue to happen. The problem is that whoever creates the tension, doesn't always feel they are doing so or perhaps worse may even enjoy. They don't even feel there is tension. In this book I'm not dealing with the latter. My focus is more on the way these topics enter into our workforce. How these topics can often have impact while being Black in Corporate America.

In Corporate America, minorities walk away often saying "I can't believe this happened" or "You'll never guess what they said today" or "they just don't get it". I've often heard people say "they claim to care about the professional development of minorities but we're still the last and least promoted".

All in all I believe that just like within a marriage before you can move towards a healthy relationship someone must acknowledge that you're "off course" and that they can contribute to making things better. Just like with the above-mentioned victims someone must acknowledge there was preventable wrongdoing instead of trying to justify what they did. Similarly, in Corporate America, companies, HR departments, CPO's have to look in the mirror and self convict. They have to say things like "does this org. chart reflect who we claim to be?" or "Let's study the percentages of our minorities being promoted" or "the best way to get more minorities into our organization is to treat those that are currently here well". By doing this it makes your company look more appealing. It tells me that I would be rewarded for my performance. If I come in and do a great job I can move up the ladder. I can feel this company isn't afraid to promote its minorities as I can see with others that are currently here.

Repair

I think the next thing that needs to happen is for companies to go into "repair mode". This means making an obvious and serious effort at resolving the problems. This effort must be seen by everyone and should be visibly obvious to both sides (employer and employee) of the organization.

In my *Healthy Marriages* book I described repair as: "Repair – What can you do, action-wise, to fix the situation and avoid it the next time? Keep in mind that ‹faith without works is dead' [James 2:20, King James Version (KJV)]. What can you do to resolve it? If you work outside the home, you may have made a mistake on a task, or in a conversation. A good leader will ask you, ‹Okay, this happened. What can you do next time to make it better?' That's all you're doing here. Part of repairing a misstep in a marriage is a sincere apology to your spouse with a promise not to repeat whatever you did. Root out the cause and eliminate it. Progress may not be 100 percent, but a consistent effort can be".

It's too often when our nation hits a bump in the road, like the moment we're in now, with all the racial tensions and the "Black lives matter" movement, all companies want to do a public display, that they're sensitive to issues at hand. HR departments begin putting in extra hours. All the minorities in the company are "tapped" on the shoulder and asked what things they can do? Or some even go as far as asking the employees "how are you feeling?" Some companies corral all their managers in an effort to have sensitivity sessions relevant to the subject matter. To the minorities it looks like the company has gone into a "let's be nice to them mode". Sometimes the company will address their position at the national meeting. I've seen Senior VP's get up on stage and emotionally cry over the situations or they will talk about their lifelong Black friend that they grew up with. A lot of minorities (including me) feel this is the weakest effort to portray and that it's all reactionary. Some companies will go as far as spontaneously invite all the minorities on stage to share their feelings.

We're all waiting on the REPAIR. What are we gonna noticeably do to make it better? I recall that once a good friend of mine was up for a promotion on his job. He had been passed over on three prior promotions to people with less experience than him but he kept applying for positions. The time was around the killing of 17-year-old Trayvon Martin. The country was in a racially sensitive mode similar to today (BLM movement). He was at nearly 20 years in with the company and with good consistent performance ratings. Another person going for the position was a person with seven years experience (and while it should not matter this person was a White female). She was a very strong performer within the company and considered to be on a performance fast track to success. They had just recently attended a regional meeting and were expected to hear who would be named the next general manager (the position they were applying for) of their area.

It was at this meeting that the attending upper management team were super friendly to all the minorities. The meeting facilitator kicked the meeting off with a message of hope to all minorities. He even said "all lives matter in our organization and we value the contributions and efforts of our minorities". They were asked to stand in front of everyone as he acknowledged each one of them and some were even offered the mic if they wanted to share their sentiments around what was going on around the great racial divide of the current events.

Shortly after the meeting it was announced that he didn't get the promotion. She had. This was puzzling because here was an opportunity for the company to do the right thing if indeed he was valued. This was another missed opportunity for the company to show "Black lives matter".

I'm not saying that because of the death of Trayvon Martin Blacks are expected to be promoted. What I am saying is for companies not to use the racial issues as their platform to publicly announce where they stand but then not back it up with any actions. A good repair would have been to promote him.

He had more experience, he was mobile and he was capable. This was his fifth position he posted for and her first. I'm sure there could have been other determining factors but without any explanation and considering all things equal this was a missed opportunity at an effective repair in my opinion.

ABCnD's (Communication)

The next thing I talk about in *Healthy Marriages* which I feel is applicable here is the ABCnD's of communication. This is simply having that conversation in an effort to resolve the issues. It's not an argument. It's not a blame game. It's most definitely not a one way conversation. ABCnD's referees to becoming "A Better Communicator in Dialogue". This is an effort on both parts to seek understanding, alignment and resolution.

The design is to communicatively put you in a position to be comfortable to openly discuss where the disconnect is and what can be done to prevent it from recurring.

"Being a Better Communicator in Dialogue is about improving how you communicate by applying basic rules of equitable conversation. It comes after the two pre-dialogue steps, but will be a third action you take in addressing any of the principles.

When we know we have to address a complicated topic, we take an approach–avoid stance. Some tend to avoid the discussion whereas others may whine about what they don't like. Neither is an effective pathway."

"Most of us don't like conflict, (especially at work) so we put off such a conversation hoping to avoid any confrontation. We don't want to burn our imaginary bridge, nor do we want the other person to hurt us—and I'm talking about injurious conversation.

Hurt feelings happen when we gravitate toward sentences starting with,›You did this', or ‹You did that'. It sets up a blame cycle putting the other person (normally the subordinate) on the defensive. When someone feels defensive, he or she can't move forward. Emotions escalate, people make statements they don't mean, and the parties walk away worse off than when they began. Some people even quit their jobs.

If we avoid that approach, we may try resolving a problematic situation by engaging in a monologue rather than a balanced exchange of ideas and perceptions.

A monologue is when one of you does all the talking. The manager or HR usually dumps all of the reasons the employee missed the mark. This exchange reduces the level of comfort to have such a discussion in the future.

The employer may identify an issue, view it and outline a resolution without once taking a breath for input from the other person."

"Successful resolution stems from a proportionate dialogue. Each person has a reasonable opportunity to express one's point of view. To become A Better Communicator in Dialogue (ABCnD's), follow these steps.

As you approach your conversation try to always know what your Goal is. Know what you want the conversation to accomplish. Always realize there may be obstacles within the flow. Realizing this in advance reduces you from becoming defensive when you hear something unexpected. Be sure to create a positive picture. Envisioning it going well can only help it to go well and can also help keep you on track with the subject matter. Always think before you speak. Only talk what is helpful and inspiring to the situation. If it's not fact or true it's best to stay away from it. Go into any conversation prepared to be a good listener. Ask sincere clarifying questions.

If you're the employee these steps apply. If you're the employer, they still apply. The only difference if for you to help create an environment for such a conversation to occur. The employee shouldn't feel they're gonna be targeted for bringing up such a topic. Remember, they're only looking for advice, support and quality feedback that can help them to a better outcome next time.

1) Stay calm. High emotions brought into any conversation are fruitless.
2) Ensure optimal timing. Don't press for immediacy if either of you is distracted. You want a focused dialogue. But don't let the issue fester. Plan for the exchange as soon as possible.

3) Remain on topic. It's tempting to deflect an uncomfortable subject by bringing in past issues. All that does is escalate a conversation and create further resentment. Stay on task.

4) Stick with dialogue. Seek one another's input and perspective. You don't have to adopt the other's point of view. In exploring a repair, all you have to do is recognize the other's perspective. In today's terms, this is "we can agree to disagree".

CHAPTER 1

INTRODUCTIONS

This book is written from the perspectives of three African American men who worked in Corporate America for a nearly combined 100 years. I'm one of them and you already know my story if you've read *The Reinvention of OJ Smith From Ghetto Streets to Corporate America*. To summarize I am a retired sales director with The Hershey Company. I spent nearly 30 years selling a product that was fun, sweet and consumed by everyone.

During my time there I held various leadership positions within several US markets. I developed lasting strategic relationships with customers across the country. Some of those relationships have even carried into my retirement. I've always managed to advance and develop these strong and effective business relationships. I worked for a company that allowed me to think out-of-the-box, which opened the door to creative and strategic relationships with several professional sporting teams such as the St. Louis Cardinals, St Louis Rams, St. Louis Blues, Texas Rangers, Cincinnati Reds and Cleveland Indians. Perhaps my greatest attribute is my magnetic personality and my ability to motivate and develop internal talent and external customers. I had a great run with a great company that valued my talents and skills.

Skip - works currently for a Fortune 25 company. He is as sharp as they come. Extremely smart and he "gets it." He knows how to adaptively and intellectually play to various people.

I met Skip while in college at Kent State. We both went on a job recruiting trip where there were several students from different schools. He and I have stayed connected since that time. Skip has worked for his Fortune 25 company for 33 years to date. Skip is well thought of in his company and like me has held several different positions in various markets. Unlike me, Skip has even had a three year international assignment over in China.

Skip is what I call a "keep it real brother." Many times we've helped each other through our experiences while being Black in Corporate America. Although Skip is a Senior. Director with his company he has been passed over on multiple promotions and could easily be a VP, Senior VP or even a Divisional President. To date, these are the three positions Skip still aspires to reach. Skip shares numerous experiences similar to mine. Many with different outcomes while some with the same outcome. Unlike me, Skip is an outstanding golfer and enjoys the game. He feels sometimes his athleticism is the reason why he's made it as far as he has with his company.

Clint - works currently for a Fortune 150 company. Clint is an area manager and has worked in Corporate America for 35 years. I call Clint the wisest of the three of us simply because of his tenure, wisdom and experience. Clint has never made it past the manager level with his company. He has often posted for regional manager and even a divisional manager role but never got them. The problem is, during his earlier years, he's been passed over numerous times. Even when he aspired to climb the corporate ladder, was willing to move anywhere within USA and willing to do any job. The other problem is he is the one that trains his region and divisional managers. All have been promoted beyond their level of management. This means another new manager for Clint to train. Many times the managers are half his age, not as loyal and not willing to go the lengths Clint would. Deep down inside I know Clint hurts over the stagnation in his career development but at this point he has decided to focus on his retirement. Clint often says the most memorable and hurtful thing in his career was when a young White and newly promoted regional manager said to him. "They told me to make sure I get trained by you to do my job, if I want to move far in this company." This was meant as a compliment to Clint's knowledge and skill sets but it also hurt because he had applied for the same position numerous times. In Clint's company of nearly 100 area managers, Clint is 1 of 4 Blacks. During his entire 35 year tenure there's never been more than four and even more frightening, no area manager has ever advanced beyond that level.

I met Clint during my early years at a non related business function. For three to four years I had two close friends on a similar career path as me within Corporate America. We talked often then, realizing the similarities between the three of us. I told Clint about Skip and Skip about Clint. Then I introduced the two to each other and the three of us have stayed connected even till this current day.

The Confederate Flag

For many Black Americans, especially, the confederate flag is a symbol of decades of racism, hate, violence and White supremacy.

In my opinion the main thing about the ABCnD's is the fact that you can feel comfortable discussing the tough and usually forbidden topics. You feel a level of safeness asking the questions that would ordinarily stay bottled up inside and go unanswered. I recall once asking a White teammate of mine (who was from Mississippi) a question about the confederate flag. I asked, "if we we're going to eat lunch somewhere in Mississippi and we got to the restaurant and saw a mass display of confederate flags all over the place, should I be concerned for my life?" To which he responded "I would never take you there." I then said, "Let's assume you didn't know what it looked like till we got on the inside." He then said, "No, they might look at you funny but no one would mess with you." Deep down, I didn't believe him.

Similarly, I asked the same question to another co-worker who was from Arkansas. She responded "Yeah, I would fear for your safety. It's unfortunate that some people feel that strong but yeah you'd be in trouble if you walked in such a place." I believed her.

The fact is that actually happened to me once early in my professional career. I was a supervisor training a new representative. We both were African-Americans. It was the middle of the day and we had decided it was time for lunch. Although it was her new territory she wasn't too familiar with the area. We both walked into the restaurant (name unknown). I recall it was a dark, low lit, bar like restaurant. There were confederate flags all over the wall and the clientele appeared to be bikers based on their attire. We both knew immediately we didn't belong there and backed out of the door as soon as we had walked in. I heard laughing as we rushed out and I heard "You see the pop eyes on that boy?" Followed by more laughter. We both knew we'd be the only one's in our company we could share this experience with. No one else would believe such a place existed.

Today, there's a lot of talk regarding the confederate flag and it's meaning. There are many people who say it represents a significant part of American history. I totally agree with that. Where it gets tricky are the different perspectives within that history. The other day I was having this very conversation with a good hearted White friend of mine. He actually owns a confederate flag. He says it's folded and put away as he would never want to offend anyone. I can get down with that. I just shared with him from my perspective what it means. For me there are four basic things I always remember whenever I see the confederate flag.

1) The American Civil war 1861 to 1865 was fought between the northern states loyal to the Union (who wanted slavery abolished) and the southern states that had seceded from the Union to form the Confederate States of America. They wanted the continuation of slavery. During the many battles fought, if the south won they would plant the confederate

flag on the ground of the battle as a sign of victory. If the north won they would plant the Stars and Stripes flag. I wasn't around during those days but I wanted to see more Stars and Stripes vs. confederate flags.

2) It's often said by some White people, "Well I'm from the south and it was our flag way back then..," To that I say all my family is also from the South Alabama and I assure you they want no parts of the confederate flag.

3) I look at the murders of Blacks in the 50's and 60's. The church bombings. I look at the Little Rock 9 and the opposition they faced when they tried to integrate education in Arkansas. I look at the courthouse during the Emmit Till trial. I look at opposition to federal investigators who were trying to solve the case of the three missing (killed) civil rights workers in 1963. In all of these scenarios the confederate flags were used to display the most aggression against Blacks. You don't have to take it from me. Look at the pictures for yourself.

4) I look at Klan rallies and Nazi rallies. In addition to their banners there's also the strong presence of the confederate flag carried by their members.

So you may never have any of those intentions. But these are the images carved in my head when I see it.

College Roommate

Perhaps I was at my very best with the ABCnD's during my collegiate years (freshman year in particular). I had two White roommates. Both were from all White environments and I was from an all Black environment. We would always openly and comfortably engage in healthy cultural difference conversations. The flow would always be out of a curiosity for the other's way of thinking. I can't begin to describe how helpful this became as a tool to draw us closer to each other. It was as if we were both little kids seeking to better understand each other's background.

I think this played out best as we were approaching Easter weekend during my freshman year. I shared this story in my autobiography and called it

"Guess Who's Coming to Dinner."

As Easter was approaching, Jay, my roommate, who knew a little bit about my situation (I had no place to go and was prepared to stay on campus during the extended weekend break) asked what I was going to do.

I'd planned on staying in the dorm, but he wouldn't't hear of it. He said, "Why don't you come home with me?"

Mixing cultures on campus was becoming more normalized but mixing cultures in someone's private home could have mixed results, ala Sidney Portier in the 1967 classic "*Guess Who's Coming to Dinner.*" I didn't know Jay's parents, or too much about him, so my response was immediate. "No way man. You're a nice guy, but I'm Black. I'm fine staying here. But thanks anyway."

He wouldn't't let up and asked, "What difference does that make?"

"I don't know too much about you, dude, but I figure you live in an all-White neighborhood and I'm not down with what could happen there."

He kept pushing with sincerity and I started feeling guilty for digging in so much. I was basically accusing him and his family of treating me poorly without really knowing. If it wasn't all right, I don't think he would have been so insistent, so I caved in.

I recall leaving a note on his desk that read *"Guess who's coming to Dinner."*

Looking back I think I was more uncomfortable than he was. This was my first experience in this kind of a situation and I was definitely out of my comfort zone. But I reminded myself that one of the reasons I had decided to go to college was to see what existed outside of the ghetto. This turned out to be perhaps my most favorite and memorable experiences. This would not have happened had we not comfortably practiced the ABCnD's. We were ultimately Better Communicators in Dialogue.

Just imagine what barriers this could break down within Corporate America.

It seems to me that there will always be "The Good Ol' Boys Network." This is where you are purposely excluded. Sometimes you are constantly reminded you don't fit in. You may not even want to fit in but that's ok because you're not "getting in" even if you wanted to. Of course you're included with the necessaries and the essentials of work but it's the social networking, the comradeship, the lunch cliques that remind you.

Sometimes it's the topic of conversations that remind you.

Take for example an African American in today's work place. You may be invited to dine with the "good ol' boys" but they're gonna make sure the topic of conversation is something that's gonna be unpleasant for you. They may bring it up why they feel the BLM (Black Lives Matter) movement is worthless. Or they may start talking politics automatically assuming you're not politically in sync with them. Perhaps one of the most popular things they do is they may invite you to sit with them, but as you near the group you hear some whispers then a laugh and then a welcome. It's as if they've said something about you, laughed in agreement and then have you sit in.

We've all experienced this more times than we can count. Almost as many times as the purse clutch. Sometimes it's intentional and other times it may not be. However, we notice it each and every time. This next section is appropriately titled:

The Good oL' Boy Network

Skip had been recently promoted to a director level with his company. This wasn't the first but it was one of his earlier meetings in his new role.

This was a meeting with Senior Leadership facilitating and it was located in Vegas. This was an all week meeting. During the four days they were to discuss business, customers, products, people, and on the fifth day they were going to compile and summarize the topics. Skip was comfortable and proficient in each of the areas even though he was new. At his previous position many felt he knew enough to be a director. As it is now he's a Senior director and many feel he knows enough to be a VP or even divisional president.

During the middle of the week the team had planned to do an offsite dinner. Skip had been noticing the good ol' boy network in action. Of course he was the only Black of 12 participants with a host of senior leaders facilitating. Skip noticed early the different silos and chat cliques. He shook it off thinking he's the rookie of this group. With each day he began to notice more and more odd behavior. He approached three peers who quickly disbursed when he got to the group. During lunch he noticed the senior leaders at a table while his peers split three tables. Each time there was no extra chair or seat saved for him.

A couple of times he'd just pull a chair and make space with himself but then the group would quickly change their conversation. Some members would even excuse themselves from the table saying they're gonna call home or get a smoke before their meetings resumed.

One day Skip selected a different group to try and "break into." He noticed as he was walking over to the table a couple of the members looked over at him, said something to the group, then there was loud synchronized laughter which lasted till he got there. This was odd and Skip even humorously said, "If it's that funny y'all gotta repeat it so I can get a laugh." Everyone then spoke, "Hey, Skip. What'd you get to eat?" "Here you can have my seat, I'm about to call home."

One night the group had an offsite dinner. The good thing was that the setting was with two tables that accommodated the entire group. There was no need for Skip to try to fit in. Conversation flow seemed normal most of the time except occasionally the group would focus on Skip. One would ask him a direct question and the group would silence themselves as if they all wanted to attentively hear his response. Once he responded the group would then go back into their solo clique chatters which often excluded him.

After dinner it seemed obvious the night was a wrap. This particular night there were two senior leaders with the 12 directors. They all made it clear they were going back to their rooms to turn in early. No late night cocktails, no cigars by the lounge, no hangout playing billiards. As they returned to the hotel everyone hurried to their rooms. Skip did the same. After being in his room for nearly 30 minutes he decided to go downstairs to get a snack and beverage from the concession store near the hotel lobby.

Skip saw his confirmation. He saw his "Good Ol' Boy Network'" in full action.

He saw the 11 directors and the senior leader all piling into a couple of unmarked taxi minivans. They were going somewhere. It was obvious they didn't want to include Skip. It was obvious this had been previously discussed and planned. They never saw Skip as he saw them and he never mentioned it to anyone other than Clint and I.

This was another solid reminder of being Black in Corporate America.

CHAPTER 2

THE MAIN INGREDIENT

The next portion of this book is what I'm calling "The Main Ingredient." In my opinion, here's where a lot of companies "miss the mark." This is also where some companies really do well. I believe all companies should want to do well in these areas. This would assure good, positive race relations within the organization. I believe this is valuing diversity at its best. With these ingredients the most effective outcome is when the employer works with the employee to achieve racial equity.

Corporate Credibility

This begins with the integrity of both. The employee and the employer. Who we say we are should be who we actually are. It should be who we want to be. This should be obvious to any and everyone. For example, what if I was perceived as a very fast paced worker who was always serious but I was trying to be a laidback, slow and careful paced worker with a huge comical sense of humor. Neither is right or wrong but there's no integrity to my credibility. Ultimately, I want to be seen by others as I'm trying to portray myself.

Throughout my professional career, whenever it was time for my performance evaluation I would always hear things like "You're impactful, you light up the room… people gravitate towards you," and "You're very good with people, the customers love you and think highly of you." This was important to me because that's who I was trying to be. That's how I viewed myself and that's how I wanted others to see me. Think of the miss if I heard "You're very shy and introverted."

Now, lets imagine the employer and their corporate credibility. If you're a company who constantly professes you're the best place to work and more specifically the best place for minorities and you foster none of the above (self conviction, repair, a conducive and safe environment for the ABCnD's to exist), watch out. Your corporate credibility will be crushed. If you see yourself as a great place for minorities but they see you as the opposite, that's a major disconnect. If you believe minorities feel appreciated and supported and they feel the opposite, your corporate credibility is crushed.

Let's be clear again I'm referring to your corporate credibility with your minority workforce not to your business overall. I believe most companies do an outstanding job with their business needs and thus their business corporate credibility is outstanding.

In fact, many employees will sacrifice how they're treated just to know they are working with a great company. I believe this why the best companies score well in both areas. Their external business practices are great and they don't quiver when it's time to do the internal 360 degree review. That's the review where the subordinate has the opportunity to provide constructive feedback to the management team above them.

The 360 degree reviews are good and bad (in my opinion) and here are some reasons why;

    * Good, because they give the leaders a chance to hear from the bottom and how they feel about how they're being led.

    * Bad, because there is no true anonymity and many, if not most, subordinates feel they may be targeted if they tell the truth.

* Good, because if they are in an environment where constructive criticism is accepted that can lead to monumental resolutions. It's a simple as listening to the internals and reacting. It enhances the corporate credibility (as long as something is done about whatever's not working).

* Bad, when the subordinate is confronted on why they feel how they feel.

* Bad, when the team of subordinates are called into a meeting and asked to redo their assessment in an effort to generate a more favorably accepted response.

* Bad, when a subordinate is put on performance probation shortly after their input has been submitted. Often times this can appear in a form of "Well they were sub-par performers anyway." Even if their performance was subpar, terminating an employee after a 360 degree review seems to be bad timing because that employee will always walk away feeling "Once I submitted my feelings" they fired me. It also gives the company an opportunity not to address whatever was the disconnect described in that particular employee's feedback.

* Good, when the leadership addresses all the feedback and work to collaborate with the subordinate to resolve the issue then seek follow up feedback in that area. This is where most people (minorities) feel a huge lacking. The company will hear you, there will be no retaliation but there will also be no follow up to the matter at hand.

You get the idea.

Someone recently shared with me they were (are) currently up for job promotion. They are with a Fortune 500 company within Corporate America. They are African American. There's another African American with more tenure also up for the same promotion. The two are good friends and would be happy if either of them gets the job.

During the BLM movement the company reached out to both as most companies do with their minorities asking them for their candid input as the company is concerned about their minority workers during this racial divide. The company commended them both on sharing their sincerity regarding how they're feeling as minorities in Corporate America. Both expressed their feelings when passed over on promotions. Both expressed the company has an opportunity to "do good." My friend expressed if they didn't get the position due to the other person, they'd even be comfortable being the "backfill" for that person. They both felt good that the company was paying attention to their needs.

A few days passed and one of the two asked about the status of the posting and was told "We're pretty close, we're just waiting on an approval from HR." Later that same day the other was told "We got the approval we were waiting for from HR. We will be reposting the position."

How do you think that made them feel?

What do you think that did for the corporate credibility of that company?

To date, neither have been told why the company felt they need to repost the position and what they were lacking that prevented the company from moving forward with either of them.

Where's the integrity of the company after having that "Black Lives Matter" meeting?

Corporate America, how do you see yourselves? How do your Black employees see you?

In this last example, I bet there's a major difference.

Character Intention

Character Intention is when you have a genuine concern and care for people and you try to show it. This doesn't mean you hit the mark all the times but everyone can see your intentions. You invest quality time in seeking a mutually beneficial ground. This isn't to be mistaken with false intentions. False intentions is when you show interest in public but there's purposely no necessary action to follow up. It's a lot of talk but then the action gets canceled. Or the actions get postponed again and again until they are no longer a priority. It's when the main reason for showing the genuine concern is all of a sudden forgotten and now you're repeating whatever disconnections you've always had.

The other day a friend of mine contacted me. We both coached sports together and served on a school board at the same time. We had a very laidback conversation while sharing perspectives. My Black perspective and his White perspective can mix and merge especially when we want the same things. We invested over three hours just talking about COVID-19, the racial divide in our country and about our families. We both were acting in the best interest of each other. Neither was inclined to put our thoughts and understanding above the other. Shortly afterwards he called to share with me some of the actions taking place as a result of our conversation. I'd say that was character intention with a genuine concern and effort.

We knew that we could both be candid and honest about our intentions. He wanted to have a trusted and different perspective regarding the BLM movement.

Again, both our intentions were genuine, it's just that our background approaches and experiences were different.

I feel this is one of the most awesome and effective demonstrations of Character Intention. I feel as though whatever decision and input he shares from our three hour lunch conversation will add more value since he's not just basing it on how he sees things.

His plan was to not only collaborate with me but to get perspectives of other minorities.

To me if this was done more often in Corporate America the landscape for *Being Black in Corporate America* could be impacted even more favorably.

It's very obvious his intentions are not to push his agenda. He was seeking a more collaborative effort with his approach to his business situation. I shared with him my "scrambled eggs" analogy.

Imagine this (most companies do this), while seeking the world's famous Black man's scrambled eggs they praise him, bring him in to meet the boss, ask him how he does it. They ask him so they can make the "Black scrambled eggs;" they'll even give him the credit for the eggs. They'll even feature him as they serve the eggs. He may even get a pay raise and bonus for sharing his information.

Instead of asking him how to make the scrambled eggs, why not promote him as the maker of scrambled eggs in the company. Or the supervisor, manager or even director of those making the scrambled eggs. During this racially sensitive time in our country I'm hearing a lot of companies connecting with their minorities to ask them how to make the scrambled eggs, or how to lead the diversity and inclusion efforts or how to help them assure the minorities are happy.

Think back to our last story of the two who were up for the same promotion only to learn that after the company had the racially sensitive meetings with them they decided to repost the position. Did this company do their best to demonstrate their genuine concern for these two tenured and loyal employees?

Capable - KDM shot calling

Perhaps the most important part within the Main Ingredient is when a company has that KDM (Key Decision Maker) that exercises their authority and makes the big call. Many times I've seen situations where there's that one person in a company who could (like Thanos, from the Avengers Infinity War) snap one finger and make things right. Go back to the scrambled eggs example, there's a person that can easily say, "That's it. We're gonna make you our director of foods, you'll oversee the scrambled eggs moving forward amongst other things." How often does that happen? How often should it happen?

Let's look back at the two African Americans going for the same promotion.

There should have been one capable KDM in the position to say, "Listen, while we're in the Black Lives Matter era plus we just called employees in and told them how much we valued them. We also asked them to help us get this right. We also told them how much we valued their performance and their loyalty and felt fortunate they were both candidates for our job posting." Surely that person could have said, "The right thing to do is to promote one of them into that position. This will strengthen our *Corporate Credibility* with them. This will also be a *Repair* to what they sincerely told us was an issue. This will show them and others we were listening. This enhances our *Character Intention*. We are who we say we are, who we want to be and we are how we want them to see us." This is an ultimate example of that KDM making one call and resolving an issue while preventing a process to interfere with progress, consistent with the credibility of the company.

I recall this happening once with Skip. While at a national sales meeting. The CPO asked him "How are things going?" He said, "great." She then probed deeper and said, "No, really how are things going? How are we doing?"

The two had a trusting, open communicative relationship. She had shown him she was sincere with her intentions and she valued his perspective since he was African American in a predominantly White Fortune 25 organization. She even sensed there was more to his "great" response. She said, "Let's have a cup of coffee." Then said, "Now tell me, how's it really going?" He felt comfortable to be really transparent, as he'd always been, with her. Not in a complaining and whining way but in a diplomatic and respectful way. He then said, "I know for dinner tomorrow evening we're planning to go to the Historic Civil War re-enactments resort. I know they do re-enactments and I totally understand it's a part of our history. In fact, I know that history very well."

She then said, "Well, what's the problem?" He then further explained, "I don't feel comfortable in that environment with some of the people at this meeting. Some are culturally sensitive but then there are some here that are not culturally sensitive and with alcohol in the picture I don't want to overhear someone say something out of line."

She said, "If you hear that, let me know. I will be there and will deal with it swiftly." He then further explained, "I don't want to turn into the company snitch. I already know there are people unhappy with me as a director and the last thing I need is to be the snitching director which would give them even more incentive to be against me."

She empathetically understood his position. And said, "I get it" I never thought about it like that. "How do you think other minorities feel about this?" He said, "I know for a fact there are several that are equally uncomfortable but they're not on the level I'm on and don't feel as comfortable talking "up" within the company." She then offered to host a meeting and take the ten minorities to have lunch there the following day, followed by a meeting to assess their feeling of the location and dinner plans.

The next day (day of the planned dinner) a group of 10 were gathered with the CPO and other members from the senior leadership team to openly discuss the feelings and concerns about the dinner plans. The meeting was authentic, sincere, intense and transparent. The outcome was six were uncomfortable and four were willing to attend but it wouldn't be their preferred plan for dinner. The CPO then made arrangements for the group to eat lunch there that day just to get a feel for the place. After the lunch that day all ten minorities had reservations about the dinner plans. Each understood the historic significance of the location but each also had a concern for possible insensitivity from peers and co-workers. Two people thought it might be a good idea to allow the minorities to sit together to avoid hearing any insensitive chatter. Most thought that would not be a good idea and would create more internal separation and possibly some hostility.

The CPO took the stage after the last session of the day (approximately 3 hours before dinner). She empathetically announced she had decided to change the dinner plans. In the most eloquent way she rhetorically asked, "Imagine if it were you and you didn't feel comfortable." She then said, "Instead of going with our original dinner plans we will be doing something more fun. We will be going to the amusement park. All details have been handled. Your admission bracelet will get you unlimited meal, any restaurant or food stand throughout the park." And just like that, at the snap of a finger the plans had been changed.

Obviously, there's more to this story but the main point here is that this CPO empathetically listened, took action and adjusted plans because what she heard from Skip when she asked, was a genuine concern. This is the ultimate example of a KDM calling a shot. This exemplified a self-convicting moment, which also led to a repair of what could have been a damaging moment. This demonstrates *Character Intention* and enhances *Corporate Integrity*.

Visible Results

Visible Results is the actual measurements of our past and current performances. This is the part that makes it easy for people to believe simply because they've seen it before. Expecting it to happen again is not such a long shot. Visible results is actually getting the right things done with everyone witnessing. Think of the last example with Skip at the national meeting and the CPO made an instant adjustment that accommodated the minorities attending. That situation enhances trust with her. This doesn't mean that she's gonna always deliver a favorable outcome for Skip and other minorities, but I'd be quick to trust she would before I'd trust any other person or situation because she's done it before. She didn't do it behind closed doors. She didn't secretly do it. She wasn't anonymous about it. She delivered visible results.

As we think of the employer being empathetic to all employees, how do you think she saw herself? How do you think minorities saw her? There's likely a connection and consistency with how the two saw her as being empathetic. As being a KDM who can call the shots no one can argue that she clearly positioned herself as that person. As the person who could and would take responsibility for results.

Let's look at the "scrambled eggs" example. With the scenario where the company asked "how to do it" I'd say there were no visible results simply because if they didn't get it right, people may say "they listened, tried to emulate but it's still not right." On the other hand, if they promoted the Black person to the director level he/she could then oversee and assure the scrambled eggs were made right. They may even open up new opportunities that may be well perceived. This move to promote the minority could alone be considered a *Visible Result*.

Right ALL Wrongs

Right All the Wrongs is simply, making things right (with the quickness) when they've gone wrong. Think about an unarmed shooting of a Black man which has happened too many times and too recent. It's bad enough that the shots were fatal but what's even worse is when justice seems to drag its feet with arresting the officers, charging the officers, acknowledging the wrong that has been done. Many times it's the delay in the justice system that sparks the movements. Many Blacks (and I'm one of them) feel that when a White officer fatally shoots an unarmed Black man, there will be no charges, no admission of guilt or wrongdoing and justification as to why the officer feared for his life when the unarmed Black was running away from him.

Righting the wrongs calls for a quick apology. That alone demonstrates some sincerity. To deny or justify the wrongs will almost always create a protest and reaction.

It's fake, or lacks sincerity, or more importantly makes it hard to believe we're trying to get better when there's a cover up or when we try to hide our mistakes instead of repairing them.

Let's look at the example of the two minority employees posting for the same promotion. The company talks to them and tells them how valuable and how much they matter. The company then reposts the position. That's a wrong that needs to be corrected. Most of the times it goes unaddressed. The employees may never know why the position was reposted while they were within the process. They may think, "What's wrong with me?" "Why are they reposting? Do they have someone else? Do they want someone better? Do they really value me?" These employees can walk away feeling like they're dealing with counterfeit instead of authenticity. In this example the Fortune 150 company has a chance to right a wrong because this situation is still current.

I believe Corporate America misses this so often. Sidebar conversations that occur are sometimes out of line. Passed over promotions without helping the employee know why they missed or perhaps are not qualified seem to linger so long until the employee changes jobs.

In June of 2020, there was a lot of talk of the celebration of Juneteenth especially in the news. As explained by some Whites it's the celebration when slaves were freed. The meaning is actually deeper. Slaves were freed with the Emancipation Proclamation in 1863. Some states like Texas decided not to tell them. Texas slaves were not notified of their freedom until June 19, 1865. Thus Juneteenth is when (those slaves who had been withheld knowledge of their freedom) celebrated their freedom.

President Abraham Lincoln's signing of the Emancipation Proclamation had officially outlawed slavery. However, in Texas and the other states in rebellion against the Union almost two-and-a-half-years earlier enforcement of the Proclamation generally relied on the advance of Union troops. Texas being the most remote of the slave states had a low presence of Union troops as the Civil war ended; thus enforcement there had been slow and inconsistent before the official announcement. Although, Juneteenth generally celebrates the end of slavery in the United States, it was still legal and practiced in (Delaware and Kentucky) until later that year when ratification of the thirteenth amendment abolished slavery nationwide in December.

Transparency

Creating Transparency is when you tell the truth in such a way people can verify it easily. They don't have to wonder if what you're saying is truthful. You present yourself with "nothing to hide." Think of some church pastors. When they deliver their message they're standing behind an acrylic clear glass podium or some are standing behind a very thin podium. Then three are others with no podium at all. This is their way of showing there's nothing to hide. In many cases this builds an immediate trust.

In the 70's one of my favorite songs was "Whatcha See is Whatcha Get" by the Dramatics. This song implied "I have nothing to hide, I'm as real as how you see me."

In Corporate America it would apply there's no hidden agendas. "You can expect what we say will come to pass."

Let's look at some examples we've already discussed. With the two African American employees applying for the same position there clearly was no transparency. First they were reached out to and shared how valued they were. They were asked to lead an effort sensitive to the BLM movement in an effort for their company to be on a good track with its minority workforce. They were both told how valued they were as loyal, professional and hardworking employees. Then they were told the company was gonna repost the position they had posted for. That's not being transparent.

Transparency could have been promotion of one of the two. Or, perhaps transparency could have been calling them (individually) into a meeting and giving some advance notice that they were going to repost the position and why they felt the need to do so with them being candidates for the job.

Let's look at the national meeting with Skip and the CPO. Perhaps the ultimate display of transparency. Once the CPO empathized with the minorities she immediately reacted on their behalf.

Too often too many companies operate on hidden agendas. Especially when it comes to minorities. We've all experienced this at some point. Sometimes it's major and other times it's minor but we've all seen this. It's often referred to by the minority as "two sets of rules." This implies what works for some doesn't work for me.

Clint was once at a leadership meeting with his Fortune 10 company. After the meeting there was a happy hour which meant an open bar. Clint noticed one of his peers had too much to drink and was getting out of hand. He knew if this had been him he would have been written up or verbally reprimanded (as he should have been). With this person everyone ignored the remarks coming from him. Everyone seemed to laugh at the obnoxious behavior from him. No one felt the need to "harness" the situation for the sake of the company's reputation. Clint's assessment was that for him and other minorities the podium is acrylic and clear. It cried out no such behavior will be tolerated. For others the podium was large and wooden, which was loaded with hidden meanings and lots of cover up. This podium prevents the reality from being seen or is the hidden meaning the actual reality? Two sets of rules.

Straight Talk

Straight Talk is as simple as it sounds but is often too difficult for the company to have with the minority employee. Straight talk is being honest. Telling the truth even if it's unpleasant. Or keeping it 100, which is to say 100% authentic. Call things what they are. If your company will never have a Black VP, director or senior leader then don't give the minorities applying to work there that impression. Don't tell them the "sky is the limit." Don't manipulate people or distort facts. Don't leave false impressions. Straight talk would be more like. "We've never had an African American excel to this level but we'd like to do so. With your talent and skill sets perhaps you can help us break that barrier." None of the African Americans in Corporate America (that I've spoken with) have ever heard anything encouragingly similar.

Straight talking is similar to the American Constitution and the Civil Rights Movement. Whereas the Constitution states men of all races, nationalities and all creed are free and created equal; yet in many places and for many years the Black man didn't experience this. It says all men, which includes Black men. It doesn't say some men but it says "all men." The social difference and segregation was nothing near straight talk for Black men. The late Dr. Martin Luther King, Jr. describes it as "America having a schizophrenic personality classically divided. On the one hand she has proudly professed the noble principals of democracy and on the other hand she has sadly practiced these principles."

I recall once going on a recruiting trip with another recruiter who was White. Because we were visiting HBCU (historically Black college and university) we had taken two African American entry-level reps with us. We walked into a room where we were gonna talk about the features and benefits of working with our company. We were going to invite those interested to our interview session on the following day. Before we even could get started I recall one of the students saying, "Can we have him (referring to my Caucasian counterpart) leave the room? We'd like to have some real talk." I knew exactly what he meant. As soon as the room was cleared and only African Americans were in the room he asked, "OK, lets keep it 100. How far can I advance in the company?" I recall responding something like we're a company that promotes from within and we're always looking for the next leaders of the organization. Then another student asked, "How many of us are at your level? And how many are above you?"

Regardless of how I responded to that, talking straight "cuts to the chase." We were not going to lie or deceive. We weren't going to spin the truth or leave them with false impressions. Either our answer was going to be powerfully impressive or similar to many companies. The difference was the fact that there was no podium to hide behind and this class was going to get the truth. And they did. There was no beating around the bush. There was no double talk. There weren't even partial truths, which leave the wrong impression. It was at that very moment, no matter what we said, the most important tool of truth was the historical performance of the company. It would be obvious if their *Corporate Credibility* was strong. There would be obvious and visual examples of *Character Intentions. Visible Results* could easily be drawn from our responses to their keeping it 100 questions. What mattered most from us was our Transparency and our Straight Talk.

I've often thought and said the best recruiting tool for any company is within the results you've posted. That makes it clear for everyone to see. We can bring in all the minorities at the entry-level we want but the best story to tell is how well the current minorities within the organization have been treated. Treat what you got well and you'll get all you want banging on the door to get in.

CHAPTER 3

CHOICES

O ften times these experiences play a role in the choices we make while working in Corporate America. I don't mean the day-to-day operational choices I'm talking about those choices that we think could help us be seen as more favorably. Things that may have the company stroke our ego.

I recall Clint having just had one of those moments. He had been introduced to a new supervisor. A much younger White male who appeared to be really trying hard to impress. A person who Clint felt should have been behind him for the same position. Clint had 7 years experience and the new supervisor had 3 years. Clint is currently still with the company and that very supervisor lasted a total of 5 years.

This occurred as Clint was in his car which was parked. The supervisor came over to say farewell for the day and patted Clint on the head. As if he were a pet. Clint quickly corrected him by telling him, "We don't do that in my culture. Please don't put your hands in my hair again." Clint wondered if the choice to correct this supervisor would have any repercussions.

Shortly after this a Senior Vice President was coming into the marketplace to have dinner with the team. This will be called the **2001 MM Dallas dinner**. This event occurred on February 2001. Clint would have been included in that dinner of approximately 15 other people. This was great exposure to Senior Leadership. This was that KDM that could snap that finger and make things happen. Clint had been passed over multiple promotions and thought this could be a positive opportunity for him. His annual business outlook was very good at plus 30%. His January performance was strong at plus 25%. The month was February, and he was down 11%. However, his quarterly outlook was at plus 25%. This meant he was going to make up his deficit and finish strong for the quarter and into the year.

This night Clint made the choice to sit next to a VP. This VP was notoriously known for finding one person in the group and really cutting him/her down. He was an ex-marine. Clint felt it wouldn't be him because he had a strong and positive business outlook besides, he was the only Black person at the dinner that evening.

As everyone seated the VP asked them to share their name, market performance and outlook for the year. Clint was sitting directly next to him on the left.

He went third. He said his name, then identified his market and his to date performance. Before he could share March and the quarterly outlook the VP cut into him. Clint knew immediately he was going to be the goat for the night. Appetizers hadn't even been served. People were laughing at him. Some felt bad for him. The VP was not letting up.

Such comments as, "How can you be here tonight when you haven't made your month?"

Then he'd say, "This is what we don't need, he comes here with a big smile on his face wanting to get a free meal but isn't delivering results." Some at the table chuckled. This cut down went on the entire night. Clint never fought back, he took it like a man. He had seen this torment before but it just didn't seem to last this long. It just didn't seem to include the personal sarcasm.

Clint never touched the appetizer, his salad, his meal was untouched. Even his dessert was untouched. All he could manage to do was take a few sips of water to show people he was still alive. He even recalled a couple of times where the servers chuckled at him. This was embarrassing and humiliating. All night long during this two-and-a-half hour dinner he wondered when he will move on to something else without coming back at him. At the end of the dinner as everyone was getting up to leave the VP leaned over to Clint and whispered, "You chose to sit in this seat." Clint left that night wondering if he would still have been the target had he sat in a different seat. Perhaps that supervisor who left had shared with the VP what Clint said to him after he had patted his hair.

Perhaps the most hurtful thing from that night in Dallas was that as the first quarter ended and the middle of the year closed, Clint hit his projected numbers as he predicted he would. He finished Q1 plus 25%. He finished Q2 plus 37%; finishing each month within the second quarter at plus double digits. He thought perhaps that VP would acknowledge this. Perhaps that VP would say something like, "I beat ya up hard at the Dallas dinner but what a performance. Here's an example of thick skinned delivering the results." He never acknowledged Clint's efforts. Clint finished the year at plus 31% as he had projected. All done with no acknowledgement.

Choices can make or break us. That night, the chair Clint chose to sit in hurt him inspite of his strong annual business performance. I'm often reminded of the choice the late great Motown RB singer Marvin Gaye made when he went against the plans of Berry Gordy, as he wanted to record his *What's Going On* album.

In June 1970, Gaye returned to Detroit where he recorded his new composition *What's Going On* after he witnessed acts of police brutality in Berkeley. Upon hearing the song, Berry Gordy refused its release because he felt the song would be "too political" for the radio. Gaye made a choice and responded by going on strike from recording until the label released the song. *What's Going On* released in 1971, and reached No.1 on the R&B charts within a month, staying there for five weeks. It also reached the top spot on the pop chart for a week and reached No.2 on the Hot 100 chart, selling over two million copies. At least, in this example, Gordy came back and publicly announced he was wrong and gave Gaye his proper due.

National Meeting Breakfast 3Hard Way

I recall once being at a national meeting and it was breakfast time. I've always been very popular and could have sat at any table with anyone and held a good conversation while having breakfast. This particular day I walked into the dining area with two other African American male employees. Both were well-tenured with the company, and we had developed a great friendship over the years.

As we entered the dining room, one said, "Well I guess it's time to split and find our group to dine with." I then said, "No, there's an open table for four. Let's sit there. We shouldn't have to split up from sitting together." We did just that. We sat together at an open table for four. There seemed to be a silence, perhaps some whispers but we were each comfortable sitting together that day. As we went to the buffet line to get our food and return to our table we began small talking about nothing - talking as you would if you were eating with friends. After all that's exactly what we were doing, having breakfast as friends. We weren't discussing business. We weren't plotting a big attack. We weren't rebels. We weren't rebelling anything. We were simply having breakfast as friends and we just all happened to be Black.

I recall thinking to myself, it's gonna be a "brave soul" whoever takes this fourth seat at this table. If it's another Black person, surely it'll be someone who's comfortable being Black unlike the stairwell hello dude. It'll be someone who makes no apologies for being Black. On the other hand, if it's a White person that sits in the chair it'll be someone who's culturally comfortable. Someone who's not threatened by the presence of more than one Black communing. Either way, it's gonna be a courageous move for someone to take this seat.

Just as I was thinking those very thoughts a White manager came to our table and asked, "Is this seat available?" We all said yeah and welcomed him to our foursome for breakfast.

This is how it should be. I count multiple positives with this experience. As three Blacks in Corporate America, we were comfortable being ourselves and staying within our Blackness. The company environment wasn't going to interfere with us communing as three Black men. There was someone brave enough to come and dine with us putting himself in the minority situation. I'm sure there was some discussions going on as to why we sat together that day but if that situation arose again, I'd do the exact same thing without hesitation.

National Meeting, sitting together...

"Break it up"

I recall my friend Skip facing a similar situation with a much different outcome.

He had attended a national meeting somewhere in Florida. Probably into the third night of the meeting after dinner, several African Americans wanted to meet others outside of their working market. You may often hear of people but because you're not working in the same market you never get to meet each other. On this night they had decided after their dinner they were going to have a few cocktails. It was probably around 10 to 12 individuals. They grabbed a table that would accommodate them all. Skip was the highest ranking Black in the company. He was a Senior Director; you would think if he's around there's a lot of respect for his authority. After all, many aspired to get to his level although many also knew he was capable of even doing more.

It was the norm to have a dine around after dinner. Normally, it was almost recommended in an effort to mix and mingle outside of one's normal working environment. "Get to know others," networking is what they called it. In Skip's mind he knew this was a "cutting edge" thing. He also knew there could be some resistance. Some Whites in Corporate America feel a threat whenever they see a number of Blacks assembled. I'm sure we've all experienced this to some degree.

After dinner was over they did just that. They assembled at a table as a group. They were all excited to finally meet people they had never seen before. They were extremely excited because they all knew of Skip and his professional reputation. Skip was very well thought of. If you ever followed his career path it was always good things you heard about him. The group wasn't being loud or standing out. It looked like a simple and normal gathering. There were groups gathered all around the pool area.

Some groups of three, some of five to seven, some even of just two and several groups of 10 or so.

All of a sudden an SVP (Skip's direct supervisor) walked over to the area where Skip and the African Americans had assembled and said something like, "What's this? Let's break this up." Then he leaned over and whispered to Skip, "This isn't a good look."

Which company do you work for? What would your company have done? If you're an SVP and you saw this assembly would you have broken it up? If you would not have broken it up would you have felt uncomfortable that minorities have assembled?

Companies, this is a great area to assess - Are you who you want to be? Or are you perceived as who you actually are. I'm sure Skip's company would say they have no issues with its African Americans but yet this night they demonstrated the very opposite.

Be Yourself - Don't change the radio...

As I said earlier, I've often thought and said the best recruiting tool for any company is within the results you've posted. That makes it clear for everyone to see. We can bring in all the minorities at entry level we want but the best story to tell is how well the current minorities within the organization have been treated. Treat what you got well and you'll get all you want "banging" on the door to get in.

Sometimes the problems within corporate America is "Us." We're not comfortable being who we are. We sometimes are over gracious because they've allowed us exposure to their world. We sometimes are not proud of our Blackness. As for me, I love being Black and I'm always proud being me. I've always said, "I'll make no apologies for being myself."

The late singer "Godfather of Soul" James Brown recorded a song in 1968 titled "Say it loud, I'm Black and I'm proud." That's how I feel whether in Corporate America or at home or wherever. In my last book, you heard me talk about always finding the inner city ghetto of any place I've gone and even walking those very streets. That's me. That's who I am. That's where I've come from.

Like I said earlier, sometimes the problem with Us is Us. Everyone isn't proud of where they've come from to get where they are. Of course they say they are but the first opportunity they have to pull away from their Blackness they do so. I recall once early in my career, I was a sales representative. I worked for another CPG company before I started with The Hershey Company. I was still learning how to "walk." My supervisor was going to work with me. As I picked him up in my company car I had been listening to my music on the radio. Probably R&B, Jazz or Reggae. When he got into the car I adjusted the volume down so it wouldn't interfere with any conversation but I didn't change the radio station. The radio stayed on all day during our work (or ride along as it's often called). I recall at the end of the day as he gave me feedback for the day he said "I notice you never changed the radio station. Always find out what your supervisor likes then adjust the station." He then said, "I like country music" as he exited the car not waiting for a response.

It was several days before he was scheduled to work with me again. I recall constantly thinking about how I would address this with him. Finally, the day came where he was scheduled to work with me again. This time as he entered my car, I turned the radio off completely. I never changed the station but I wasn't going to listen to country music all day. I actually like country music and even have a respectable country music collection. But this was about me not conforming to who he wanted me to be in my car.

That subject never came up with him again.

The Stairwell "Hello"

Skip recalls once being at a meeting in the corporate office. By this time he had been promoted multiple times. He was a Director by title. There was an African American male he'd see in passing. He worked in the corporate office. Skip had seen him before and had often spoken to him with a slight, soft response return or sometimes without a return response. I never really thought much of it. Skip figured he didn't hear him or perhaps he was just socially shy. On this particular day Skip decided to take the stairs versus the elevator up two flights. As he was going up the stairs the dude was coming down the stairs. They were the only two in the stairwell. He spoke to Skip as if they had been long lost buddies. He seemed to be at such ease speaking. He had a smile on his face unlike all the other times Skip had seen him in passing.

I recall thinking to myself how odd that was. Perhaps he hit the lottery and Skip was the first person he ran into after being notified. Perhaps he was carrying some bad news on his shoulders each of the other times Skip spoke without a response. Skip even jokingly mentioned to him, "I've seen you numerous times and even spoke to you but I'm not sure if you heard me." His response was something like, "They don't like seeing us gather, so I just keep to myself and move on."

As we concluded our chat I recall thinking how disappointing it was to hear that. That is exactly the opposite of being Black and proud. I can't even blame that on the company. Deep down that's a mentality many Blacks have. We sometimes feel it's not ok for us to be seen together in a predominantly White environment especially if it's at work. I'm sure he felt that had he spoken to Skip all those other times the company would have told him that wasn't permitted or would have not allowed him to walk the halls if he were also on site and walking the halls.

Perhaps some companies foster that atmosphere but I know mine didn't. The bigger concern is that this is the perception of many Blacks working in Corporate America and we all know perception is a reality.

Companies, this is a good area to assess with your minorities. Dialogue around what's their comfort level communing as African Americans. They'll either say they feel comfortable doing so or they will say they feel all eyes are upon them. This will sometimes lead to the choices we make as African Americans within Corporate America. Especially, when we are in positions of leadership.

Being the ONLY Black

Another thing we deal with is being the "only Black" in the environment. This doesn't mean we're the only Black in the company or in the organization. Perhaps because we are the only Black manager, attending the monthly managers meeting it's our perspective versus theirs. Our perspective or input can often be looked at as odd since it's a minority perspective. Then what happens next is we tend to "shell up." That means we are less willing to share our input because "no one else gets it."

A friend recalled once being in a meeting. They were brainstorming on a particular direction to move forward. My friend remembered saying something like, "Why don't we forego the last route then adjust at route 7, then we can move north from there." Dead silence. Not even a word to the suggestion she had just made. The very next response came from a White counterpart.

He said something like, "I think we can move north if we just adjust at route 7 and forego our previous route." Immediately there were cheers of acceptance. "What a great idea," "that's the kind of leadership thinking that landed you all in this room, great idea."

I wish I could say this was the first and only time this sort of thing happened but it seemed to be a regular occurrence. One you get used to. When making the recommendation my friend would no longer look for acknowledgement of her inputs. She had grown immune to this sort of behavior.

My friend Clint once shared this experience. He and several managers and senior leaders were on a market tour. This is when several people tour the market where their product is distributed to see an actual pulse, to see customer and consumer actual reactions to the products. This would often give them ideas of what things could help, and what things might be interfering with sales. This tour would often include marketing executives and other senior leaders who would normally not see what's happening at "ground zero."

This particular tour consisted of 11 people. All but Clint were Caucasian. This one day they toured an inner city market in Boston. As the team of 11 was leaving a store an African American male from that neighborhood greeted them. Had it not been 11 of them they probably would have been afraid of him. They probably would have been afraid to even assess that market had it not been 11 of them. As they were leaving the store the guy said, "Wow a bunch of White people in our area, something is about to go down, wow." Then as he saw Clint he said, "Aw yes, and here's the token Black." The group laughed as his comments were humorously made. The hurtful thing to Clint was being the "token Black" and the extra hurtful thing was the laughter of his teammates and the laughter of his Black brother. It was at that moment that Clint realized he didn't know how he fit in since both sides were laughing.

Companies, are you sensitive this could be a typical day or feeling for some of your employees? I'm not even sure I know the best way to deal with such a thing other than just being empathetic. Again, I'm just trying to share some very common experiences some Blacks deal with in Corporate America.

CHAPTER 4

Listening with a third ear

Listening with a third ear simply refers to hearing something but then determining the true meaning or intent behind what was actually said. We've all heard a comment or statement made and wondered what was the real intent of the comment.

Skip recalled once working with a tenured subordinate. He was driving and Skip was on the passenger side. This employee and Skip had a fairly decent relationship but he would often say things that would make you wonder what were his motivations. Perhaps he wanted a promotion he didn't get. Perhaps he was uncomfortable having a Black manager. Or perhaps our brain is just working overtime when we hear what we hear, which makes us wonder why we had to hear it.

As they were driving along the two-lane highway with another 40 miles of drive time ahead, a truck pulled up beside them. It had a decal in the window **POW-MIA**.

Skip softly whispered Prisoner of War and before he could finish what he was about to say (Missing In Action) the employee blurted out Power of White Men In America. Skip said to him, "Wait, what? I always thought that stood for Prisoner Of War - Missing In Action." He responded, "Maybe to some, to others it means Power of White Men In America".

I went through my mental Rolodex wondering what would make him say that.

What was the message he wanted to relay? "Why didn't he just keep that thought to himself?" I know to this day I believe it means Prisoner of War but I scrubbed every source I could find to see if there was another meaning. Whether it is or isn't, it sure had me wondering. I wonder more what made him plant that seed in Skip's thoughts. Did he just want Skip to know how he was thinking?

Companies, this isn't something I would turn into a debate. This isn't something to write him up over. This isn't something to run back and tell my superiors. It's another example of hearing something that you know is out of corporate character but you know you heard it and you wonder what was the real intention behind hearing it. It makes you wonder what if others feel this way. What if the roles were reversed and I was the subordinate and it was my superior manager that made the Power of White Men comment.

I recall very early in my career when I had recently been promoted - my first job promotion. I was a supervisor. I was pretty excited for my new role. I now had people responsibility and I recall having lunch with another friend who was also in the CPG industry. We worked the same territory in similar job roles. He was in beverages. On this particular day he shared with me, "This week in particular is rough because two things happened within one week in my new role. The first was my manager (two levels above me) called me into his office. On his wall was a **confederate flag**. He asked does this bother you? I said no, but I do realize the confederate flag represented the South during the Civil War. I realize the South wanted slavery to continue and the North fought to abolish it. It doesn't bother me I just now know where you stand." He then said, "I'll take it down because I don't want you ever to be offended. I had another employee in and asked him the same question. He said yes, it bothers him." I thought to myself, "If you know it offended the first guy why wait to ask a second guy?" My friend then asked me, "Don't you think that's odd?" As much as I agreed I just felt fortunate to not have had that experience.

The second situation, my friend recalled "Was the fact that as soon as I was announced the supervisor one of my employees resigned. I had met her once. She seemed like a pretty nice lady. She had been with the company for quite some time so I figured she just decided to retire. While working with another employee of mine the conversation came up as to why she left. Naively, I thought nothing of it until the other employee remarked you know the real reason she left don't you? I said no, why. She then explained, 'I knew her well. In fact she trained me when I was a new hire and I've been here 10 years. She told me she just couldn't do it.' Puzzled, I asked, 'Do what?' Then she said, 'Work for a Black.' My friend then said, wondering why she had to spare him the details 'and how about you? Are you gonna resign soon too?' She said, 'No, I don't think that way. I just wanted you to know what you're dealing with.'" I recall not seeing that dude around much longer. I always wondered if he just couldn't take it or if he got promoted again.

Companies, I don't expect you to know how each and every employee thinks or feels about race relations. However, I do think many of your minority employees' deal with this kind of stuff on a regular basis. It may not be a bad idea to periodically assess the true culture of your organization. Many times when Blacks commune in the workplace it's simply to innocently release this type of tension. This one week told me more about the company than anyone could have attempted. I absorbed it as a norm within our country. I could look beyond individuals and see that I was beginning my career with a great company.

I believe every company needs to know this is common culture that exists and your minorities have probably experienced it to some extent. They will probably never tell you but they will absorb and deal with it. However, some may decide another company is better than yours.

Another similar situation that makes us practice listening with a third ear is "this Job is not the right fit for you." I recall during one of our group chats Skip told us that sometime early in his career he was up for a promotion.

At this time you were "tapped on the shoulder" when you were going to be promoted. There was no posting process. Yes, it was all subjective.

He felt confident that he was well-qualified and had groomed for this new level of responsibility. He had been told by his superiors he's ready. He had been getting great reviews and his confidence was at an all time high. He was even told by his direct supervisor to "get ready, your days in this market are numbered." It was as if the world knew he was going to get the next promotion.

Skip was expecting the next opportunity to become a district manager was going to be his. He imagined how they would tell him. He imagined what market would he be in. He was internally excited that he could be soon going anywhere in USA to continue his climb of the corporate ladder.

The next position that became available was in the Boston market. Skip thought for sure this would be his next opportunity. Hours went by, no phone call. Days went by, no phone calls. Days within the presence of his supervisor went by and the topic never came up. Suddenly weeks had passed and there was no mention to Skip about the Boston assignment.

Finally, Skip decided to bring it up with his regional manager (who was two levels above Skip). This was his boss' boss. Skip firmly asked, "Why didn't I get asked for the Boston assignment?" He was told in a "matter of fact" tone, "We would never do that to you. That job is not the right fit for you." Skip asked, "But I thought everyone said I was ready to be a district manager. I know I'm more qualified than the last three promoted." The manager then nodded "There's some real backwoods thinking and we didn't feel that would be placing you in a position to succeed."

Skip did get the next promotion, which was in Detroit - an even larger market. The irony to this story is that many years later Skip did eventually get the Boston market and worked with the customers identified as "backwoods thinkers." He had an exceptional relationship with the customers and business hit record numbers.

Companies, have you ever done such a thing? Let's count the many infractions here. I wonder if there was any **Self Conviction** from Skip's managers who thought they were doing him a favor. With no self-conviction, there's certainly no room for **Repair.**

Perhaps the biggest miss here was the **ABCnD's** in communication. How much time elapsed with Skip just wondering why he wasn't being asked to go to Boston. Especially, after all the hype he'd been given. **Character Intention** - is this who the company really wants to be. Perhaps the company can say he did get the Detroit position but does that really **Right all the wrongs**? I don't think so. The problem is this kind of stuff happens all the time, again and again. To the company it looks like they're taking care of their minorities. To the minorities it looks like two sets of rules.

Act 1, The Marishalota

This next portion of the book all pertain to three experiences I had. No reflection on the company I worked for. The problem was they each happened while I was on the clock - while I was at work. They are significant to me because one minute I was in Corporate America mode and the next minute there was an occurrence or something would be said that would remind me I was actually Black in Corporate America.

The **first** is what I call the **Marishalota.** I was a supervisor working in the Cincinnati market. This is after I had realized one of my employees resigned because she said, "She couldn't work for a Black." I recall working with an employee. We had a good working relationship. I had actually hired her to replace the lady who "couldn't do it."

She was the driver and I was on the passenger side. We arrived for our first appointment for the day a few minutes early. We decided to wait in the car until opening time. This would give us time to discuss the sales plan for the day and for this particular call. While it should not matter I recall wearing a suit and tie to work every day and especially on this day. We couldn't have been in the car for more than 20 minutes before there was a knock on her window from a police officer. Simultaneously, a knock on my window from a second officer demanding me to get out of the car. His gun wasn't drawn but his hand was on his gun and he was ready to draw.

I obviously complied and exited the car trying to explain who I was and why we were there. I felt obligated since I was the supervisor and she was a relatively new employee of mine. I was told to shut up and his partner asked my employee, "Mam, are you ok"? She said, "Yes." Keep in mind it's approximately 8 a.m. on a Wednesday morning, I had to "assume the position." As I was being frisked the officer asked my employee again, "Are you ok?" He then implied "You don't have to be afraid, we're here to help." I felt so degraded and embarrassed for me. She finally convinced the officers she was fine and we were there waiting on a store to open. Apparently someone had called the police saying there's a Black man assaulting a White woman in her car. That's what the officers explained to us.

This is one of those incidents I would not have told anyone; especially anyone at work. She saw firsthand what it was like for me trying to be a Black supervisor in Corporate America. I believe she was embarrassed for the experience and we joked about it afterwards but I did ask her to please not mention this to anyone. When she asked, "Why? You did nothing wrong." I explained I don't want any sympathy over this, as I'm sure it may not be the last time something like this happens.

The **second** such experience is what I call **Ft. Wayne Dinner (mongoloid baby)**.

At this time I was a district manager with the company. My confidence in team management was pretty high. I knew my superiors thought a lot of me. I was now managing full- and part-time people. I was also the manager of a supervisor.

I recall once having dinner with a subordinate female. Having dinner with my teammates is something we often did whenever I was in town. Sometimes I would even have them invite their spouses. Other times I would not obligate them to leave their families and come out to dinner. On those nights I would just stay in my room and order room service. The subordinate would normally select the restaurant location simply because we'd be in their hometown and I was just in town to work with them that day and would likely work with other local employees causing me stay over two maybe three nights sometimes.

On this particular night there was going to be three of us for dinner but the male employee couldn't make it at the last minute. So now it was me and the female. We went to dinner as planned; just the two of us. I recall many strange looks as we entered the restaurant. It was a steakhouse. I felt extremely uncomfortable because of the strange looks. I said, "Hey, why don't we go elsewhere or it's been a long day we can bypass dinner altogether. You can get home to your kids and I can just get room service." She replied, "No I'm fine besides I'd like to show you the presentation I've prepared for tomorrow." I said "ok" I thought perhaps I'm racially overreacting.

As we were seated I just felt the stares even getting stronger. I just ignored them. Then I excused myself to use the restroom. When I returned I saw her face was "broken" and sorrowful. I asked, "What's wrong?" She said, "Let's go, I'm ready to go." I asked no questions and said, "Sure."

As we exited the restaurant I asked again. She explained when I left for the restroom the table of five men next to ours said to her, "Race mixing ain't good, you're gonna have a mongoloid baby."

Once again, I'm reminded I'm Black in Corporate America. This wasn't even a personal dinner this was going to be a working dinner. I do recall she was so upset that she didn't report to work the next day.

Companies, how sensitive or empathetic would you be if your employee shared this experience? As an African American manager, this is another incident I would just keep to myself. The damage was already done. This makes me wonder how many in that restaurant saw and felt the same thing the table of five good ol' boys felt. How many felt the same thing but wouldn't say anything. This confirmed I wasn't racially overreacting to stares and looks I felt that night. For that reason, I would always shy away from having a one on one dinner with a White female employee. I would avoid it if I could. If I couldn't, the image of that night and that experience always played loud in my head.

The third experience, "**Courtyard elevator, We're not all bad**" came at a time where I was a district manager. Timing was not too far apart from incident #2. I was attending a managers meeting in Detroit. We would often meet at a certain hotel, have breakfast then have a meeting for nearly six hours. I was one of five managers - four peers and our supervisor a regional manager. I had a great working relationship with my co-workers. Two of us would come in from out of town the night prior. We'd have an overnight room.

While in the meeting I recalled I had left something in my room and I briefly excused myself to get it. I recall feeling really good and fully accepted.

I had forgotten about the "Marishalota." Although pretty recent I had forgotten about the "mongoloid baby. "Once again I was feeling good as I was on my climb up on the corporate ladder. As I jogged expeditiously to catch the elevator to get to my room, I noticed there was a man and a woman already in it. Before I even got to the elevator I could hear their conversation. It was something like this, he said, "Hey did you go to the event last night? I heard it was really nice." She said, "Yea I know, I was gonna go. I went and there were too many niggers there and I just didn't feel too comfortable so I turned around and left." It's at this precise time I entered the elevator. With only the three of us in, the door slid close and the elevator preceded to go up. Then he said, "I know exactly what you mean and I don't blame you at all." Then there was silence and 10 seconds seemed like an eternity. The elevator got to my floor, as I exited I said, "We're not all bad." I often wondered how they reacted or responded. I was so crushed. Once again, realizing even as a manager, dressed professionally, while at work adding value, I was still viewed as being Black in Corporate America.

When I returned to my meeting someone asked, "Are you ok?" They could tell I had been gutted by something even though I tried my best to just shake it off.

Companies, if an African American had brought these events to your attention how would you handle? What would you do? How do you think the person wants you to handle? I'm sure many of your minority employees have their own stories. You may never hear about them. They may cut into the individual's heart and yet s/he will choose to keep it to her/himself probably because they don't feel the authentic empathy can exist.

CHAPTER 5

Knowing What Progress Looks Like For Minorities

In my opinion, this is an absolute "must know" area. Imagine being at a national meeting. You have a new CPO on board and this is their first time meeting the company. She was the replacement to a "KDM Shot calling CPO" described from the previous chapter. As she takes the stage there are some questions asked of her. One of the questions is, "Do you feel this is a top place of employment for minorities?" She responds something like "I don't know what makes this a top place...." I'd say "time out! time out! time out!" Skip experienced something similar. You gotta know what the criteria is if you want to be a favored place of employment not just for minorities but for any employee.

I recall being on a diversity panel once and I was asked a similar question. "What does progress look like for African Americans in Corporate America?" I responded,

"When we are paid equally."

When African Americans are among the highest paid (for example if you look at the top five salaries in your organization, how many are of African Americans?).

When the percent of African Americans being promoted increases.

When there's African American representation at all levels of leadership within the company.

When the African Americans have effective pipelines assisting them up the corporate ladder.

When there is evidence of no glass ceiling (meaning an African American can and has penetrated all levels).

But I certainly could not, did not and would not respond, "I don't know..."

I looked at five companies which African Americans recognized as favorable places to work. These are all Fortune 500 companies.

Here are four simple benchmark numbers. If your company is better than this, that's awesome. If not, there's an opportunity to bridge some gaps.

A) Is your workforce 20% Black? Compared to the US adult population.

B) Their managers are 17% Black. I'm willing to bet there's not too many "being the only Black in the room" situations.

C) Their promotions in to management is at 32%. This clearly indicates they take care of those they've hired. That makes it easy for them to attract others into the organization.

D) Their senior levels (CEO and direct reports) are more than 10% Black.

Let's look at it on a broader scale. Let's look at all employees. Blacks, Whites, Asians, Hispanic, Indian, men or women, young or old. I'm calling this the 8 IF's.

If the following were evidently equal for everyone the problem would be solved.

IF they were paid well for what they do.

IF they had an effective mentor within the company helping them with their career path.

IF they found their job or responsibility challenging.

IF they felt they were fairly and timely promoted.

IF they constantly felt they were involved in key decision-making.

IF they were evidently and constantly reminded that they were appreciated and valued.

IF they were empowered to make decisions to help the company win.

IF they were sincerely trusted to do their job.

Companies, IF you can deliver on those "IF's" consistently with EVERY employee I'm willing to bet you'd have a top place of employment not only for African Americans but for every employee. The key is, you can't deliver on the Ifs for some employees and not everyone.

I recall Skip sharing with us (Clint and I) what he called a challenging but also hurtful conversation he once had with his supervisor. Skip was, and still aspires, to become a VP with his company. During this conversation his supervisor said to him, "I just want you to know I think you're doing a great job. You're one of the best at your level in the entire company." This was an annual performance review conversation. Skip knew he was doing a good job and delivering measurable results. He had made it clear that he wanted to eventually become a VP and ultimately a division president.

His supervisor then said, "Look, as far as I'm concerned you're the best I've got and the best I've had in this position but our SVP says as long as he's here you'll never become a VP. I don't know why he feels that way but he was pretty adamant about it."

Skip then asked, "Do you think I'm capable?" "Absolutely" his supervisor responded. "I think you're better than some to the current VP's. But he made that point very clear to me and wanted to be assured I delivered the message".

This devastated Skip. He wondered why didn't his supervisor stand up for him. Why didn't his supervisor challenge the SVP. What good is it telling Skip he's one of the best at his position if you're not going to do it when it really matters. He then went to a person he once worked for who was in HR. He asked her, "What is it going to take for me to get a VP role?" He felt she would be candid with him. She worked in the corporate office and had the pulse of many of the Senior Leaders. He also felt he could trust her. She told him you can't become a VP directly from your current role. You need to at least be at this level for 3 to 4 years.

Skip accepted this and disregarded what his supervisor said. He had been in his role 2 years and figured another 2 years and he'll try for the VP role again. Less than one month later a peer of his who had been in the same role for even less time than Skip got a VP role.

Companies, how would you handle such a thing? Who can Skip turn to? What should he do? Where's the corporate credibility?

Often times African Americans adopt the mentality that we must work harder. We must do more. We must do twice as much to get similar results as other corporate employees. This was a clear example of that.

In my Healthy Marriages book I share an analogy on success. If you ask many people what does success look like, they'd describe a straight arrow pointing upwards.

In reality success is an arrow pointing upward but it has many bumps in the road. Many obstacles. Many delays. Many hurdles to clear.

"Many times people believe success is a path always moving you forward. If you think the same way and don't view success in terms of trials and tribulations, I challenge you to reconsider your position. Imagine yourself on your way to a job interview riding an elevator in a tall building of 50 floors. Let's say you enter it for the first time, press the bottom for the top floor and it shoots right up without stopping. Most people would like that and think they were really lucky. But by going straight up, do you lose anything? I believe that you do.

Imagine that instead of going straight up, the car stopped to let people on and off all the way up. What might you benefit from that ride? You'd learn more about the building itself. You might see what other businesses are in the building. You could even have a conversation with someone in the elevator that turns out to be a type of personal or professional networking opportunity. Now you have a textbook of information. In this example, consider if something came out of your visit with the business on the fifth floor that causes you to use an immediate resource you uncovered on your interrupted trip up to the top. Which trip is the most successful? The one that shot straight up to 50, or the one that made several stops along the way?"

What does success look like for African Americans? I look at little things like TV game shows. Let's look at my two favorite game shows 'The Price is Right' and 'Wheel of Fortune.' On 'The Price is Right,' I've seen several times where two Blacks made it to the showcase showdown. Obviously, the one who bid closest without going over wins their showcase. Getting to the showcase is as fair and equitable as it can be. There's no subjective selection for who gets there. It's simply based on whoever spins closest to $1 on the wheel without going over. That's a level playing field.

On 'Wheel of Fortune' of the three contestants I've rarely seen more than one African American at a time. It appears, somewhere, someone is subjectively deciding that's not the look they want. Even if in the preliminary rounds they identify three African Americans they want on the show it appears they space them out so they're not all on together. Don't get me wrong, I love this show and watch it every opportunity I can. I even sometimes record it to assure I don't miss it. I'm just sharing my observations.

Look at the movies. In my opinion there should always be one Black actor in a major role in every movie. That makes it more realistic. That's just my opinion.

Let's look at the Broadway hit musical, *Alexander Hamilton*. There are several Black actors in the show playing a major role. In most cases they are portraying Whites. The acting and the play is so good that you focus more on the story and its delivery and not the color of the skin.

Progress looks like swift judgements. As I think of the assaults on unarmed Blacks or anyone for that matter. Swift judgements to resolve would be making progress. With Rodney King, after the video was seen by the world, everyone thought surely there would be a conviction. There wasn't. Afterwards we all learned of the Trayvon Martin killing. In my opinion there wasn't swift judgment. The problem is that many Blacks feel when there's a killing there's no swift, and sometimes, no judgement at all. That's the real problem. We often hear where the shooting officers have been placed on administrative leave. Which is to me like being on vacation.

I don't say this only for crimes on Blacks. I wanted to see swift judgements in the Reginald Denny beating. In my opinion OJ Simpson was guilty. But again, that's not what this book is about. Back in chapter 2, we talked about THE MAIN INGREDIENT. The Two Main Ingredients, that would apply in these scenarios are *Right all the Wrongs* and *Visual Results*.

Dimensions of <u>MY SUCCESS</u>

This next portion of the book is dedicated to all young minorities working in Corporate America, and are striving to climb that corporate ladder. In addition to all your talents and skills you already possess, I would highly recommend being proficient in the next few areas this book will discuss. I feel anyone who's strong in these areas will do nothing but help themselves move ahead.

The first is a triad of dimensional behaviors that I'm calling the 3 I's - Initiative, Impact and Integrity. Let's begin with **INITIATIVE**. We will define this as being proactive. Making active efforts to influence events to achieve a positive goal. Being a self-starter versus having to be told or directed all the times. Of course we all need guidance from supervisors but once you have the map and you know the objective there's much you can do on your own to accomplish the goals. This is the person that takes the appropriate actions to achieve the goals. This is the person that often goes above and beyond what is required.

This is the person that is often identified as doing more than what's required without being asked. This is the person that is constantly generating ideas for improvements. It's vitally important how to harness and share all of this initiative. Oftentimes companies can see you as a threat. They can say you don't listen and you're on your own agenda. You want to be the person that will immediately have a solution for the problem without being asked. This is the person that is also opportunistic. Think of baseball. The team needs one run to win or tie the game. There's a base runner but he's not yet in scoring position (2nd base). The base runner needs to get into scoring position. He may steal second without getting a sign from the dugout. The risk is being thrown out but the reward is being called safe plus being in scoring position plus helping the manager keep the team in a position to win. The ultimate reward is if the batter gets a base hit while the runner is in scoring position, now the game is tied or the winning run scores or you've drawn closer to your opponents lead.

The rewards clearly outweigh the risks.

If you can be this person at work, especially while being Black in Corporate America you put yourself in position to be more successful. As a supervisor, manager and even director this was the dimensional behavior I'd look for when interviewing candidates. This told me that once the person figured out how to do the job I would not have to "hold their hands" they'd know how to get to the "finish line."

The next is **IMPACT**. Quite simply, making your presence known and remembered. This is the person who "lights up the room" when they enter. All of a sudden all eyes are upon you. Your confidence and your positive energy is radiating. People want to be around you. This person carries himself confidently and is perceived to be a very knowledgeable and interesting person. This person can create a good impression without even saying a word. They command attention. This can be demonstrated in what you wear and what you say and even how you say it.

The next area is **INTEGRITY**. This is always going to be a must. People must sense you are honest to your word and that you're trustworthy and believable. I used to hear that in sales -people buy from whom they like. I used to add to that, "and they like who they can trust." Whether internal or external you need people to believe you are a person of your word. If you say you're going to be there tomorrow and do it, then be there tomorrow and get it done. This person is not the gossiper. They are perceived as having the ability to maintaining confidentiality. This person fairly represents the company's plans, policies and procedures. They also represent their subordinates well. Think back to Skip and the conversation with his supervisor where the VP said Skip would never become a VP. The supervisor missed a huge opportunity to demonstrate his integrity with Skip. Likewise, this person fairly represents the interest and needs of their customers. In such a way they constantly can find some common ground to meet and exceed business needs thus creating "win, win, win" situations. That means the company wins. The customer wins and ultimately the consumer wins.

The next behavior is **PERSONAL LEADERSHIP**. This is slightly similar but different from initiative. This is the person who on their own does what it takes to make themselves better. Personal leadership has you setting and achieving the realistic goals you've set for yourself. These are goals of performance and accomplishments. These goals are always in alignment and consistent to the ultimate goals of the organization. This is the person who wants to be a contributor. This person wants to be in the game and doing well. This is the person that helps others do well as it makes them even better. This is the person that is not satisfied with average or mediocre performance especially from themselves. This is the person that's always looking outperform their last performance. They like being compared to the best of the best. They are very driven. When this drive is consistent with the drive of the company you've now become a very valued employee. It's very easy to see the high standards this person has for themselves and others working around them. Think of NBA legends Michael Jordan or Magic Johnson. As good as they were they always knew what areas they needed to improve. More importantly, they knew how to improve those particular areas. They were as good as the team and their teammates needed them to be. It's a known fact that both these players did not like sub-standard performance from anyone and especially themselves. Being a teammate around this type of attitude is infectious. You want to be your best when you're in the game with this person. This person is quick to show pride when their standards are met because they know they've contributed, the team has benefited and their teammates have also benefited. This is the person that is constantly trying to get better. Constantly trying to learn how to be their best.

I think of the performance of Lakers Magic Johnson in his rookie season in the NBA finals game 6 versus the legendary hall of fame Dr. J and the Philadelphia 76ers.

Kareem Abdul Jabbar was the league's MVP, but midway through Game 5, the Lakers star suffered a severely sprained ankle. He managed to come back in the game in the fourth quarter to lead the Lakers to victory and a 3–2 lead in the best-of-seven series. But the Lakers still had to travel to Philadelphia for Game 6 without their star center. As it turned out, Kareem did not make the trip and was listed as doubtful if Game 7 had been needed.

In Game 6, Magic played what may have been the greatest game of his career. Playing on the road, Johnson (a 6'9" rookie point guard) started the game at center and eventually played all five positions in a dominating performance. Scoring a game-high 42 points and grabbing a game-high 15 rebounds—and handing out seven assists— Johnson led the Lakers to their championship.

That's what I call Personal Leadership.

Companies, if you have someone strong in these areas "let 'em play" even if it is a Black in Corporate America.

Another area is to become proficient in establishing your

INDEPENDENCE; The state of being independent. The freedom from necessary control or influence, support or aid. The company knows you will deliver and they don't have to hold your hand. You can autonomously work effectively. You can be self-sufficient. You can stay on course without constant and immediate supervision.

They have no problems listening to your suggestions, your plans, your ideas. They know that they can trust your approach and business-winning ideas because time after time you've shown that your independent thinking is consistent with the goals and objectives of the company's winning.

Think back a few pages to the discussion of the 8 IFs. These dimensional behaviors perfectly align with four of the 8 IFs for a motivational fit between the employee and the employer.

Motivational fit is when you are consistently good and enjoy doing something and that same something is what the company is looking for in an employee.

Here's what I said a few chapters back:

If the following were evidently equal for every employee the problem would be solved.

IF they were paid well for what they do.

IF they had an effective mentor within the company helping them with their career pathing.

IF they found their job or responsibility challenging.

IF they felt they were fairly and timely promoted.

IF they constantly felt they were involved in key decision making.

IF they were evidently and constantly reminded that they were appreciated and valued.

IF they were empowered to make decisions to help the company win.

IF they were sincerely trusted to do their job.

Companies, IF you can deliver on those "IFs" consistently with EVERY employee I'm willing to bet you'd have a top place of employment not only for African Americans but for every employee.

The next area I would look for the employee to be strong and proficient in is that of

INTERDEPENDENCE; the quality or condition of being <u>interdependent</u>, or mutually reliant on each other - Capable of being depended on; worthy of trust; reliably strong. They know they can count on you. The company knows you will deliver. This is the condition of a group of people or things that all depend on each other. You depend on them to do their parts. They depend on you to do your part. The common goal is the same for all.

Think of the rookie Magic Johnson. The team relied on him filling on as the leader in the absence of Kareem. Magic relied on his teammates to do their parts in contributing towards their win. In that game while Magic scored 42, the Lakers also received strong performances from Jamaal Wilkes with 37 points and 10 rebounds, and Norm Nixon provided solid point guard play while Magic was playing the other 4 of 5 positions that night. Jim Chones played strong defense on 76ers center Darryl Dawkins, while Mark Landsbuger provided rebounding off the bench, Brad Holland chipped in eight key points.

Finally, it is always imperative to have a **STRONG DRIVE FOR RESULTS**. This is the person that literally gets the job done. This person delivers consistently, time and time again. You almost become more known for this. This person will constantly set high goals for themselves and for their working team. Their goals are always accepted because teammates know of their history of constantly delivering results. This person uses effective measurement methods to monitor their progress. They work hard to achieve and even exceed their goals.

When I was a kid my cousin and I used to play with baseball cards. One of the cards I had was Hank Aaron. Consider his drive for results. I imagine all the work he'd put in to be a constant home run threat whenever the bat was in his hands. I recall thinking his teammates saying something like "All we gotta do is get on base and he's gonna drive us home." Even though Hank Aaron played during a racially sensitive era 1954-76 even the White players that weren't keen on having a Black teammate couldn't deny him because of his drive for results. Hank Aaron retired with a 0.305 batting average, 3,771 hits, 755 home runs and 2,297 runs batted in. If you don't follow baseball stats let me tell you those numbers are magnificent. I recall seeing him play as a youngster and then meeting him in an airport as I was Black in Corporate America. As much as I wanted to talk to him about his many accomplishments I also wanted to just sit back admire a Black man that went through it all and undeniably made a strong name for himself in spite of any opposition. He showed up to work everyday and delivered results whenever he was called. We too have to have that as something people can come to know us for. Stay focused while being Black in Corporate America.

Clearly I'm not saying these seven areas are a quick ticket up the corporate ladder. It depends on the company and your playing field around you. If you're working for a company that insists on holding you back then that's exactly what's going to happen.

What I am saying is this is in my opinion putting you in position to offer the best you.

This is doing all you can do to keep yourself measurably and consistently an above average performer. I submit if you take this working behavior into the right organization, the company that sincerely values strong performance no matter what the race or gender of the person is. You will have self-driven success.

Companies, if you have such a person "Let 'em play." If I were interviewing, looking for a candidate, these would be the seven areas I'd be looking for from the candidates. If I were working in Corporate America these would be the seven areas I'd want to be my strongest and I would want the company to notice these are my strongest areas. If I were asked for my opinion on how might a person succeed in their company these would be the areas I'd strongly recommend.

CHAPTER 6

Act 2 - Seeing is Believing

O K, so here we go again. Act 2 (just like Act 1) pertains to experiences I had while being Black in Corporate America. I call these 'Seeing is Believing' because if you didn't see it yourself, you wouldn't have believed it happened. No reflection on the company I worked for. The problem was they each happened while I was on the clock; while I was at work. They are significant to me because one minute I was in Corporate America mode and the next minute there was an occurrence or something said that reminded me I was actually Black in corporate America.

The **Purse clutch.** As Black men In America we see this all the time. It happens so often that we don't even mention it. Sometimes we laugh at it, other times we shake our heads and wonder why. There are times I have purposely walked in a different direction. Like across the street or I have even gone down a different aisle in the grocery store just to save an unrealistic fear of me snatching a purse. I've often even thought, there were times where I feel as though I had more money than she could have.

I recall once walking into a customer's account with my boss and his boss. We were all dressed in suits. White shirts and ties. We all had that IBM look. We had parked nearly a block away, so we had to walk a bit to get to the customer's office. There was a storefront restaurant we walked past. A large window displayed people inside dining and enjoying conversations.

We were outside and as we walked by I recall there was a table of four - two men, two women. All Whites. One of the women was seated on the bench near the window with her purse tucked between her and the window. Had there not been any glass there it would have been wide open for me to snatch it and run. However, there was a thick glass separating her inside from me outside.

As she noticed the three of us passing outside her eyes locked on me then she immediately grabbed her purse and moved it between her and the other person she was sitting next to. I really wanted to go into the restaurant and ask, "Did you think I could go through the glass?" Or "As I'm in a suit with my two bosses, did you feel I was gonna risk it all to snatch your purse in broad daylight?" I noticed this but my two bosses did not. This goes into that memory bank of mine and I often reflect on it and break out in laughter.

The next incident I call **Airport Line Kiosk.** I was at the airport about to catch a flight somewhere. I was 90% travel in this role. I had status with all the airlines so going through the nuances of checking in and getting to the plane was very regular for me.

This particular day was a Monday. Monday's were always crowded especially between 8 and 10 a.m. There was a long line at every kiosk station. At the particular station I was in had formed two lines. I was in the actual line and these two White Corporate America men were in a second line that clearly had formed wrong. Somehow they had a few people forming behind them. Many of them quickly realized their line was formed wrong and would drop out getting into another properly formed line.

As the line moved closer I was now four people away from it being my turn at the kiosk. I could hear the chatter between the two men. It was obvious one was the supervisor of the other. The subordinate wanted to impress his boss with a quick trip to the kiosk without the long wait. They had on suits, White shirts and business ties. At this point in my career I was wearing a suit, minus the tie. In front of me was a White businessman, a White businessman and woman, and then a White business woman.

Now it's the White businessman's turn but the two White Corporate America men try to go next. They back off immediately when the man gets to the kiosk ahead of them. They seem to accept it without any reaction. Next it's the lady and the man. The same thing happened. Again, they accepted it not being their turn. The two didn't even challenge the pair. Next it's the woman in front of me. Again, they didn't challenge her but while she was at the kiosk I hear the subordinate say authoritatively, "We're going next, that's for damn sure." He said it loud so I could hear.

So many thoughts went through my head. First of all I knew I wasn't gonna let this dude just jump in front of me. I resorted back to my fighting days. You have to read my autobiography *The Reinvention of OJ Smith*. I don't want to be that guy again but this situation mentally took me there right away. As she was finishing up at the kiosk, he said it again to his boss but loud enough for me to hear, "Don't worry we're next, we've been waiting here long enough." I recall saying directly to him, "It will be a neat trick if you go ahead of me." To which he did not respond. I recall thinking, "Why did he not contest any of the three Whites ahead of me? Why did he wait till the Black man's turn to start contesting the order of the line?" I just knew that I was tired of being selected to cut in front of. Especially, since the only thing that differentiated us was the color of my skin. I was even mentally prepared to get thrown out of the airport over this. Since it was post-911, I could have even been arrested. I didn't really care. I just knew there was no way I was gonna let this happen even if he somehow got to the kiosk quicker and began entering his information, I was gonna be the next person.

I recall thinking what if those were my two bosses. Would they do something similar? Or would they self-convict and get into the appropriate line. Would they have contested the other Whites or would they have waited till I (the Black) was up, then contest the order. I don't think this was an all Whites all Black thing. I think this was those Whites and this Black. As she finished I walked up to the kiosk, so did the two. I looked him off and he backed off and once again said surely we're next. After I was done I don't know if the next person after me allowed them to go, I didn't really care. I just knew there was no way that dude was going ahead of me. I even thought had he contested the three Whites ahead of me and then me, I probably would have let him go. I really disliked how he waited till the Black man came up then started saying he was next. Clearly I know these actions, behaviors and thinking does not reflect all Whites but as a Black man in Corporate America when you run into this, it leaves a bitter taste. It doesn't feel good and it puts you in that situation where you're quickly reminded your presence is not gonna be accepted by everyone. It doesn't matter what your title, company or appearance.

Overhead Luggage Space

This next situation I'm calling the "Overhead Luggage Space." Being 90% travel I had acquired status with all the airlines. I am the type of person who likes to be the first on the plane. I like being settled into my seat as people are continuing to board, whether the plane has a first class or not; whether I'm seated in first class or not. Even if my seat is at the rear of the plane, when it's my group's turn to board I like to be the first one.

On this particular flight I was seated in the exit row aisle. The plane was a regional jet with no first class section. I had been good at light packing. All I had was my carry-on luggage and my backpack. I remember boarding the plane and quickly getting seated. I had put my carry-on appropriately in the overhead space at my seated section. As the plane began to fill up and because it was a full flight the overhead luggage space began to diminish. Suddenly, the guy who would be sitting across the aisle from me boarded.

He was one of the last to board the plane and there was clearly no overhead space in our seated area. He looked forward the plane but never towards the rear of the plane and not finding any overhead luggage space. Then he started adjusting the luggage that was already in place in the overhead space in our section as if this was going to create space for his carry-on.

Then he touched mine and asked, "Is this yours"? I said, "Yes it is." He pulled it out and put his in place then he grabbed mine and tried to find a space for it. I said, "Hey man, wait a minute. You can't do that, my luggage was already properly stored." He then came back to our section trying to find a spot for my luggage. Then the flight attendant rushed over and said, "Sir, there's no more overhead space. You're gonna have to check your luggage." He said, "Well this isn't my bag, this is his. I'm sure it'll fit." I then unbuckled and stood saying, "Wait a minute, my luggage was already there. He pulled mine out and put his in." Several seated passengers murmured in agreement with me but before I could say anything else the flight attendant harshly said to me, "Sir we don't need any hostile reactions. We're trying to take off without any delays. Now, you're luggage will be available for you at curbside as soon as we land." I tried to explain again and said, "Ma'am my luggage was..." Again, she cut me off and this time said, "Sir, I'm gonna ask you to take your seat or I will notify the captain and have you deplaned."

I was crushed. She said this even though several seated passengers spoke in agreement with me. I was crushed because the man sat across from me as if nothing involved him. I wanted to punch him in his throat but on this day I didn't go back to my St. Clair days as quickly as I did with the kiosk situation. Besides, in this case I don't know who angered me the most the man or the flight attendant. I wondered if I were White would he have moved my bag. I wondered if I were White would the flight attendant have listened to the seated passengers and made him replace my bag and check his. I wondered when he went to grab a bag was he trying to get lucky and pull the Black guy's bag. I wondered would my boss have done that. Again, this to me was not a White-Black thing in general. It was that particular White flight attendant plus that particular White passenger and me being Black in corporate America.

The Hitler Salute

Perhaps this next scenario I wouldn't have believed myself even though I saw it with my own eyes. In fact, I didn't believe it until another person confirmed they saw it also. I call it "**The Hitler Salute.**" My company had sent me to a training session. I was one of about 20 other participants and the course was taught by an outside training facilitator. This was some sort of leadership training course.

I recall the very first day in the session, it was a Monday morning and we were doing introductions. The room was set up in a U shaped format. I was right in the middle of the U and I recall there was this guy to the right of me. I just remembered he talked a lot. I can't even recall what company he was from. There were probably 10 Fortune 500 companies represented at this training session. We were all at leadership levels with our respective companies. Of the 20 participants, I was the only Black. By this time in my career I had grown used to being the only one. I had even braced myself to hear some slippage of an inappropriate remark that could be made. I was good at addressing or even deflecting such remarks. I was comfortable being me and made no excuses. At times I just didn't like being the only Black.

During the introductions the facilitator started on my right and had the person share a brief bio of themselves. They would say something like their name, their company, years of experience, where they were from, career aspirations and what they hoped to get from the session. I would be approximately the 10th person to go, based on where I was sitting.

Now, it's the guy on my rights turn to introduce himself. He said hello and his name. The facilitator recognized it was a German name and said something like "Oh German" then he said something in German, which I assumed was hello. It appeared he was showing the guy that he spoke German. Then the guy responded something in German. I imagined he said hello back. But then he saluted his left arm straight out and above his head. It was the salute I had seen on TV from Nazi's. Then I thought to myself, "That can't be what I saw." He saluted his arm and the facilitator laughed it off. It appeared that gesture even caught him off-guard and he asked him to continue with the rest of his information. I was stunned. I figured that couldn't be what I saw.

I recall thinking that was the most bizarre thing I've ever seen and because I was the only Black in the room there would be no other person I felt comfortable asking if they had seen it. I couldn't tell if there were any Jewish participants and even if I could, I didn't want to ask if that was what I saw, then be wrong, and stir up an unwanted emotion. So, I just kept it to myself. When he was done I went on and introduced myself and gave all the bio information and tried not to think anything of it.

That stunned me all day long. And I was sitting next to this dude. "That just couldn't be what I saw. But I know what I saw." Then at dinner it all came to a reality.

The group of five or six at my table were in discussion about the day, our companies and our families. Then one lady said, "Can you believe the Nazi salute?" Then another guy said, "I can't stand him. He talks too much." Then I said to myself, "They saw it too." That was our topic of discussion for the next few minutes. I wasn't going to chime in. Then the lady, who appeared to be most disturbed by the gesture said, "Someone should tell the facilitator." I then said, "If we saw it, he saw it too." As the conversation simmered down I recall someone was gonna mention it to the facilitator in an effort for him to address it with the dude.

I don't know if that ever happened. All I really cared about is the confirmation that I wasn't seeing things. My imagination was real. As sad as it was

I was not the only one to see it. I then wondered if other table discussions brought up the topic. I then wondered, "Perhaps they were all good with the gesture." I wondered if the facilitator addressed it with him. Through the rest of the seminar he seemed to remain the over-talkative annoying dude. But I never saw another such gesture from him. I do recall he and I having nothing to say to each other during the entire week. I could tell he wasn't to keen about me. Another reminder of being Black in Corporate America.

The next story is one that I probably felt was least likely to ever happen. I'm calling this;

Inability to check in: The Prestigious Hotel

This was late in my career and I was at the Director-level. We were attending a convention in Las Vegas. We were going to be there most of the week. As a company we had decided to stay off the strip at a very nice hotel near the convention center where our event was located. This convention draws thousands upon thousands of people, so reservations are at a premium. In our company, to assure we were always in the same hotel there was a VP of Industry Affairs who would always reserve our rooms. He was very good at doing this. He was a tenured person with our company and within the industry. When he took care of things it was always done right and with class.

Upon arrival at the airport there would be a vehicle waiting for us, handling our luggage then escorting us to the hotel. Perhaps this is one of the most prestigious feelings I could come to have in Corporate America. The other most prestigious feeling is having the opportunity to fly on the company's corporate jet several times. On this particular day my flight landed nearly the same time as my peers. We would meet in the baggage area, collect our luggage then connect with our driver before heading to the hotel. This was always a good connection for me because I could just listen to them and learn the pulse of the company. These dudes always knew what was going on. Of course, I would be the only Black. I'm assuming by now, you already know that.

As we get to the hotel I could tell this aura was a little different. We were in line to check in and I was next but the hotel person called for one of my White peers. I was clearly next. I thought to myself, "How could you miss me? I'm the only Black." Even my peer spoke on my behalf saying, "He was clearly ahead of me." The hotel clerk reluctantly took me. I say reluctantly because he wasn't smiling like the other clerks. Plus he seemed pissed off that we called him out for skipping over me. I gave him my credit card and ID so that he could check me in. The lady clerk next to him called my peer to get him checked in. She had a big smile on her face. She seemed pleasantly friendly and I recall thinking to myself I wished I had her versus this grinch dude.

Next thing I know my peers are all checked in with their room keys and ready to go. I was still at the desk with "the Grinch." I asked him, "What's the problem?" He then said something like "I'm sorry but we're sold out of rooms. I'm looking to see if I can get you into our other hotel just a couple of miles away." I said, "You're kidding, my reservation was corporately made months ago." He then said, "I know sir, but we're all sold out. There are several large conventions going on. Just bear with me I should be able to get you a room at our other facility." I was stunned. I was in such disbelief, disappointment and frustration. I was also a little embarrassed. The only Black guy checking in at this point and of all the people I'm the one with no room.

My peers came over and asked "is everything ok?" I explained to them what was going on and they were also in disbelief. One of them asked the clerk, "All of our reservations were made together how could we get our room and he not get his?" The clerk then explained again, "Yes sir, but we're all sold out. There's several large conventions going on. Just bear with me I should be able to get him a room at our other facility." My peer then said, "This is unbelievable. How can this happen." At this point I had lost all of my professional censors and I loudly said something sarcastic like "there must already be another Black in here and they're only allowed one at a time. This dude didn't even wanna check me in." My patience was gone, I was tired physically and I was tired of these occurrences that would harshly remind me I'm Black in Corporate America.

Finally, the hotel manager came out. All was resolved. Why did that have to happen? I had even mentally prepared myself to go onto the other hotel. There comes a time when I would much rather be where I'm wanted versus being in the most popular place where I'm unwanted. I wonder what (if anything) happened to "the grinch."

His manager should have removed him from desk duty. I'm sure other Blacks have had similar experiences. Some may have been even worse.

Companies, here's another example of what we deal with in addition to doing our jobs. This is another constant reminder of what it's like being Black in Corporate America.

CHAPTER 7

No Tolerance Zones

I've always believed, and I even still believe, that there are certain topics not appropriate for the workplace. Many companies employ this mandate but do not enforce it. I've seen and have heard of too many situations where topics have been discussed in the workplace that leads to prejudgment from supervisor to subordinate.

It can be inappropriately the topic of discussion outside of the other person's presence.

These topics are those racially charged current event topics, politics. I'm naming this section of the book **NO TOLERANCE ZONES** because such topics don't contribute to the company's performance goals. They shouldn't contribute to a person's performance but sometimes if you think the same way as your boss, they may favor you when it comes to performance evaluations.

These next five examples are real life situations that are the result of inappropriate topics of discussion within the "no tolerance zones."

1) I recall when President Obama was running for his first term back in 2007. My friends Skip, Clint and I had already discussed and agreed this shouldn't come up in discussion but it likely will. We talked about how we may be assumed to be supporting Obama simply because we were Black. We

talked about if Obama wins there could be some possible hostility. Angry Whites in positions of authority that might take it out on us.

Talking Politics (Obama vs the Tea Party)

At this time the "tea party" was a major opposition for Obama. Clint was in a manager's meeting during this time and the facilitator of that meeting a Senior VP made a comment that went something like "we don't know the impact this election will have on our business. If they get in and take over we may lose a lot of our established businesses." As he said these things Clint began to hear several sidebar conversations in whispers.

Clint was one of two Blacks in this meeting. He locked eyes with the other Black who was sitting across the room from him. Neither of them were in the sidebar whispers. This made it feel as though they were being talked about. In all actuality what was happening was they were talking about the Black democrats. Because Clint and the other minority in the room was Black the assumption was they were both democrats and Obama supporters.

One manager spoke up and said, "Yeah they're gonna take our guns away. Our right to bear arms." Then for the next few minutes the discussion had moved from business to politics. Clint was amazed how easily the subject had changed.

Neither he nor the other African American engaged in the conversation. Perhaps that's what made it end when it did. During the chatter they heard a lot of things like "those people, they're gonna take over, he's a Muslim, we'll probably lose our jobs and other cattle calling reactions." Suddenly the Senior VP observed Clint and the other lady were not engaging in the conversation and said something like "We'd better get back on track, we've got a lot to cover."

I remember Clint couldn't wait to share that with us during our next chat. Ironically, Skip had a similar experience. The amazing thing was that in both situations neither company leader acknowledged the topics were inappropriate and had nothing to do with their business plans. In Skip's meeting an HR representative was even present. In both cases they let the conversations flow and even inserted their opinions.

I believe that in both cases someone should have simply said, "This topic is inappropriate in the workplace and has no direct impact to our business plans being discussed. I respect everyone's opinion but let's stay on our topic."

The OJ verdict

This was personally painful to me because we shared the same name-sake. The funny thing about this was I actually believed OJ was guilty. But what I believed didn't really matter because I was Black and the country was so racially divided on this. One look at me and I was assumed to be in favor of his innocence.

I recall once going to a baseball game during the infamous OJ trials. I went with a subordinate of mine since our company had a small sponsorship of this team. On this particular day it was fan appreciation night. I recall as we entered the stadium fans could enter into a raffle by dropping their business card in a box. My business card read OJ Smith. I dropped the card in the box like the many thousands of fans were doing.

Between innings they would announce 2-3 winners of various prizes and have the winners go to a certain area of the ballpark to claim their prize. I recall the game was sold out so the stadium was filled. The weather was great probably 80 degrees on a Wednesday evening. It was a beautiful experience.

Then it was the middle of the fourth inning and time for more raffle drawings. The announcer called off the first name. A lady from somewhere in the stadium. The crowd cheered as if a grand slam home run had been hit by the home team to win the game. Now it's time for the next draw. The announcer announced "and our next winner is." Everyone was attentively listening and hoping their name might be called. Then the announcer said "OJ Smith." There was a thunderous roar of boos. It was so uncomfortable and unanimous that there was not one person not booing. I recall seeing popcorn thrown in disgust, people stopped drinking their drinks to join the boo chants.

I specifically recall the guy sitting to my right yelling, "Boo, kill that MF," then he looked at me as if to say join in. To the left of me was my subordinate who was the only other person in the stadium to know that I was the winner. I was the one that was supposed to fight through that anguished crowd to grab a probable T-shirt I had won. I remember seeing the thumbs down gestures normally used in the Roman cathedral when they wanted their favorite gladiator to finish off his opponent.

I tried to find the reaction of other Blacks in the stadium but all I saw were the raging fans chanting boo. I never left my seat. In fact I probably joined in with a few boos myself. I just personally declared my boos for OJ Simpson and not OJ Smith.

This reminded me how racially sensitive we were over this topic. Can you imagine if this is being discussed in the workplace the amount of suppressed emotions?

We all remember exactly where we were when the OJ verdict was announced. Skip shared with us his experience during the exact moment of the OJ verdict.

He was working with a subordinate - a White employee. The radio was on in the background. This was an employee he had worked with for years. Perhaps one of his better performers. They had a great professional working relationship. All of a sudden the radio announcer indicated going live to the courtroom to capture the OJ verdict.

She then stopped the conversation they were having and turned up the volume on the radio so they could hear the verdict. As much as Skip wanted to hear, he was willing to forego the live announcement and wait till he got home later that evening. The announcement was made - OJ's acquittal. Skip looked at his subordinate whose face was dropped in disappointment. It was as if he was sitting next to a stranger. Then she said, "I'm ready to go home now." Middle of the day, several hours remained in the working day. Skip wanted to say something like. "Let's stay focused on the job. We have more work to be done," but he knew once that verdict was announced within the "No Tolerance Zone" it was too late. They had never discussed this topic together. Her reactions made it crystal clear where she stood on the subject matter. She never even bothered to see where Skip stood. Perhaps she assumed he was in favor of the verdict. Perhaps she didn't care and just wanted to be around her own or more people that she knew were not in favor of the verdict. Either way, Skip knew a Black man trying to convince a White woman to stay when she was feeling uncomfortable was the most unpopular thing to do at this precise moment. He said to her, "Sure, I totally understand. We can finish this tomorrow."

When tomorrow came, that employee called Skip. He thought to set a time to continue their working assignment. He thought surely she had cooled off by now and was ready to move on. Her call was actually to inform him that effective immediately she was resigning from her position. Skip asked, "Why?" She responded, "My husband said I can no longer work for a nigger." Skip was stunned. He knew him. They had played golf several times before. Skip responded, "Wow I thought Bob and I were good." She said, "He likes you but he said you're still a nigger. I really like my job and I don't have any problems working with you but he wants me to find another job." Still stunned Skip said, "Ok, I understand. We can process you out on Friday."

And just like that, inappropriate topics within the "No Tolerance Zone" had affected another working relationship. Skip never told his boss all the details. He just said he felt she was in a different place after the OJ verdict. His boss responded, "That's ridiculous. No one in their right mind would let that interfere with a good job. That's too bad, I liked her. That's regrettable turnover."

Trayvon vs. Zimmerman

I recall the incident of Trayvon Martin and George Zimmerman.

Trayvon Martin was a 17-year-old African American from Miami Gardens, Florida, who was shot fatally in Sanford Florida by George Zimmerman. Martin had gone with his father on a visit to his father's fiancée at her townhouse in Sanford. On the evening of February 26, 2012, Martin was walking back alone to the fiancée's house from a nearby convenience store. Zimmerman, a member of the community watch, saw Martin and reported him to the Sanford Police as suspicious. Several minutes later, there was an altercation and Zimmerman fatally shot Martin in the chest.

Zimmerman was injured during the encounter and stated he had been defending himself; he was not charged at the time. The police said there was no evidence to refute his claim of self-defense, and that Florida's 'stand your ground law' prohibited them from arresting or charging him. After national media focused on the incident, Zimmerman was eventually charged and tried, but then acquitted of second degree murder and manslaughter in July 2013.

This quickly was another of those racially charged topics. Once again White vs Black is at center stage. Skip recalls being at a manager's meeting with a couple of peers having lunch. This topic came up. Skip was sitting with two White males. One of them said, "It's a shame what they're doing to Zimmerman for defending himself." The other chimed in and agreed. At first Skip wasn't gonna chime in. Hoping the conversation would quickly dissolve but as the conversation continued he said something like, "We just attended a session and HR talked about inappropriate topics for the workspace. This is one of those topics. Let's drop it and move onto another subject."

I'm sure he wasn't the fan favorite then but he saw no good coming from this conversation. I had recalled the OJ Simpson verdict, I had recalled the Obama for president talk. I agree with Skip and just didn't see this as being any different in terms of its racial sensitivity.

George Floyd & BLM

That was a tough experience for people to deal with whether White or Black and especially in the workplace. Let's fast forward to today with the killing of George Floyd and the BLM (Black Lives Matter) movement. There are some who believe this is the beginning of that movement. We've seen corporate leaders stand on stages and cry sorrowful tears saying how much they support the BLM movement and how bad they feel for George Floyd and his family.

Many of these leaders are the same leaders that were in place during the Trayvon Martin experience. Actually, that marked the beginning of the Black Lives Matter phrase.

So then I ask, "How does it sincerely matter to you now, but back then it didn't?"

When Trayvon Martin was murdered in 2012 and then in 2013 George Zimmerman was acquitted for his murder it generated the same uproar to Blacks then. The same as the killing of George Floyd has done in 2020. Black Lives Matter was spelled out in a love letter towards Black people by Alicia Garza. Then Patrisse Kahn-Cullors decided to put a hashtag on it and thanks to social media it took off and spread everywhere. It was designed as an online community to help combat anti-Black racism across the globe.

That's what Black Lives Matter means to most Blacks, most people. I do realize there are some good-hearted White people who have a different meaning for Black Lives Matter. I talked with several good friends of mine and they see rioting, looting and aggressive protest as associated with the movement. Well I disagree with those things also, but you have to remember that's not what Black Lives Matter is. It was designed as an online community to help combat anti-Black racism across the globe.

There are Whites that say "Don't all lives matter?" To that I say, "Yes it does." Some Whites will say, "What about Black on Black crimes?" To that I say that's another issue we face but Black Lives Matter is designed as an online community to help combat anti-Black racism across the globe. I talked to another White person who had Black Lives Matter linked to politics, gender reveal, anti-historical movement and even as a hate group. Again I say, it was designed as an online community to help combat anti-Black racism across the globe. The strange thing is he teaches his kids not to support the movement. Not to wear anything with Black Lives Matter on it. I teach my daughter that it's a movement designed to combat anti-Black racism across the globe. I teach her whenever you hear of a police officer shooting an unarmed Black man, you're probably gonna hear more Black Lives Matter chanting. The really odd thing as that both kids are school classmates who are good friends. Will this create separation now?

George Perry Floyd, Jr. (October 14, 1973 – May 25, 2020) was a Black American man killed during an arrest after allegedly passing a counterfeit $20 bill in Minneapolis. A White police officer, knelt on Floyd's neck for nearly 8 minutes as witnessed by many on a released video. After his death, protest against police violence towards Black people quickly spread across the United States and internationally. Remember, Black Lives Matter was designed as an online community to help combat anti-Black racism across the globe.

Skip, Clint and I during one of our many phone chats expressed "well here we go again." We talked about how companies would be reacting to this. We talked about anticipating what Senior Leaders would do to make African Americans feel comfortable. We talked about how some people would have a hard time understanding why Blacks are making such a big deal of this. We talked about the great racial divide that would come from this. Because Clint and Skip are still in the Corporate America workplace we anticipated the need to brace themselves. 'Here we go again.'

Clint was asked to share his perspective on the BLM movement within the workplace. He was asked to prepare a presentation directed to the Senior Leadership team. This presentation was to show the impact on business. It was to also show a positive impact on the minorities in the workplace. That is they should see the benefits for them in the workplace. It was to include one to three short-term call-to-actions for the Leadership team to employ. It was to include one to three long-term objectives (5 years and beyond) for the Leadership team to employ. The overall objective was to be perceived by the minorities as one of the best places for work for them. This was to be measured by an internal survey and feedback from employees.

Clint was given a reprieve from his normal responsibilities. He and any two other minorities he selected was to make this presentation via zoom to the Senior Leadership team. He was even told they wanted him to be "brutally honest. What's working and what's not." Clint worked on this project for two weeks. Within his report he was prepared to discuss a number of topics. They included: the glass ceiling, the percentage of African Americans being promoted, the number of African Americans passed over for promotions in the company, lack of mentorship programs, a practice of double standards that appeared as two sets of rules for African Americans and White employees and most African Americans within the company don't see a path to advancement, especially into a Senior Leadership role.

He was asked to share his presentation with a Senior VP prior to the actual delivery of the presentation; which he did.

Even Skip was asked to fly into the corporate offices and share his thoughts on the BLM movement and their company. This was to be a "down to earth, laidback candid conversation with the company's CEO, CPO and a Senior VP.

In both cases these events were canceled.

Now, let's look at three major misses just from these two examples alone. Referencing back to the beginning of this book.

Repair - Strike 1, Didn't Happen

I think the next thing that needs to happen is for companies to go into "repair mode." This means making a visible and serious effort at resolving the problems. This effort must be seen by everyone and should be visibly obvious to both sides of the organization. However, there can't be any repair because neither company has accepted the truth yet. Yes, they've asked for plans and conversations from Skip and Clint but to date both have been canceled and forgotten. To the minority employee this is something that is not forgotten at all; whether it comes up again we will always remember the lip service.

Right ALL Wrongs - Strike 2, Didn't Happen

Right All the Wrongs is simply, making things right (with the quickness) when they've gone wrong. Well this clearly can't happen because the company doesn't even know what's wrong since they've both failed to listen to Skip and Clint. In Clint's scenario it appears that once they saw what he was going to say, and how deep and "real" he got with it, they didn't want to deal with it. I think in Skip's case they never intended to hear him out. At the time they asked him, the timing was perfect. It made them appear sincere. No one would ever know they canceled the conversation.

Think about a shooting of an unarmed Black man, which has happened too often and recently. It's bad enough that the shots were fatal but what's even worse is when justice seems to drag its feet with arresting the officers, charging the officers, acknowledging the wrong that has been done. Many times it's the delay in the justice system that sparks the movements. Many Blacks (and I'm one of them) feel that when a White officer fatally shoots an unarmed Black man, there will be no charges, no admission of guilt or wrongdoing and justification as to why the officer feared for his life when the unarmed Black was running away from him.

Character Intention - Strike 3, Missed Opportunity

Character Intention is when you have a genuine concern and care for people and you try to show it. This doesn't mean you hit the mark all the times but everyone can see your intentions. You invest quality time in seeking a mutually beneficial ground.

Stop here, sentence #1 where's the genuine concern? Sentence #2, every one did see the intentions but were those real or just a façade - which is a superficial appearance or illusion of something. Sentence #3, there was no quality time invested because both meetings were canceled. If this were a baseball game, there would already be one out and now a double play takes you out of the inning. For both Skip and Clint, the double play had already occurred so this out was a major miss.

CHAPTER 8

Act 3 - Colored Man Syndrome

OK, so here we go again. Act 3 (just like Acts 1 & 2) pertain to three experiences I had and two experiences from Clint and Skip while being Black in Corporate America. I call these 'Colored Man Syndrome.' No reflection on the company I worked for. In fact one occurred while I was in college interviewing. They are significant to me because one minute I was in Corporate America mode and the next minute there was an occurrence or something said that reminded me of *Being Black In Corporate America*.

This next story I'm calling

'The Benedict.' I recall late in my junior year of college, Cedar Point offered me full-time employment once I graduated. It would be in housing, but instead of a seasonal stint, it would be year-round. They didn't press me for a decision but instead left it open-ended. I didn't know if I wanted to work for them full-time. But I also knew the job came with housing and a car, both things few other jobs would provide. In most other positions, I'd have to find housing and transportation on my own—and have to pay for them too. So now I have options.

As I struggled with this decision in my final year of college, the Kent State University placement office put me in front of lots of different companies. I had interviews with Xerox, Pillsbury and several other Fortune 500 companies. I got several job offers. Every offer was great, but each one came with a level of uncertainty—no city was locked in. For example, the letter of intent to hire from Xerox, with a salary so nice it caused my stomach to somersault in excitement, was tempting. But it said, "Your position will be in Cleveland, Toledo or Dayton." They couldn't nail down a specific location. I needed a fixed location from the start since I had to find housing and get a car. Other new graduates with more advantages didn't have to worry about these things. They had homes they could go to while they worked out various details about their jobs. I didn't have anything like that, so once I graduated, I had to go straight to where I was working.

Consequently this kept me interviewing with various companies. I recall a company had selected me as 1 of 5 finalists for three positions they had. I was the only one from Kent State and the other candidates were from various schools. We were invited to their corporate facilities for 2 to 3 days. We met with the Senior Leadership team. We had several interviews and we dined with various people in the organization. One night while at dinner, I recall the group was small this night, just the five candidates and three executives. I sat next to the CFO - they had strategically arranged the seating so that all the candidates would be integrated with senior leaders next to them.

Perhaps the strangest conversation I've ever had in my life occurred. Yes, I was the only Black. The CFO asked, "So where are you attending school?" I said, "Kent State." He said, "Oh really, I have a niece that attends Kent State. She's a nursing student. Her name is such n such. Do you know her." I said, "No I don't know her but I know Kent has a reputable nursing program." He then said, "Here's a photo of her," as he pulled his wallet from his pants rear pocket. He said, "She's easy on the eyes." I said, "No I don't recall seeing her around but Kent is thirty thousand students. What class is she?" Ignoring my last question he then asked, "I bet you'd really like to get with her wouldn't you?" I responded, "She's very nice looking but I already have a girlfriend there and we've been dating for nearly 3 years." He then said, "Look at her picture, you'd like to get with her wouldn't you?" I couldn't tell if this was a trap interview question or what. I said, "She's very pretty but I also have a very pretty girlfriend."

I know I did well with my interviews but I was never offered a job by this company. I probably would have accepted Cedar Point over this anyway. I don't know what if any impact that sidebar chat had to do with it. To this very day it puzzles me why he asked me that. I often wondered if the other candidates were asked strange and odd things. I wondered if it was just me - just the Black guy. I wondered if he really thought I was interested in his niece. I wondered if he felt all Black guys wanted White girls. I wondered what was the best way to respond to such a question. I even wondered if this company wasn't comfortable with Blacks why even spend the money and bring me in for that trip. I'm sure that's not in any manual or there's no "how to handle" this for us while being Black in Corporate America.

The next experience almost made me want to fight. I thank GOD for maintaining my professional composure. I call this:

The Property in East STL

Of all my experiences in Corporate America, this is the one that I came closest to losing my professionalism. Even more than the airport kiosk situation. I was a district manager based in St, Louis. I had just hired a new representative simply to replace a rep. I had just promoted. I was working in a rural area somewhere in Missouri with the rep. in a very small store. I had never been in this area with the previous rep. Perhaps he didn't want to expose me to the area or we had just not gotten around to it. All I know is, I was in an area I'll never forget.

I walked into the retail grocery store with my new rep. Of course, she was a White female and here I am the only Black in town at this moment. I felt all eyes were on me. I felt numerous purses being clutched. I felt like a fly in a bucket of milk. I was wearing a suit and tie but that didn't put anyone at ease. As we entered the store the first thing I asked her to do was go to the customer service booth, and meet the manager so that we can let them know who we are as we're in their store. We did just that and were welcomed by the necessary store personnel. That didn't mean we were equally welcomed by their clientele. I recall a man approached us and said to me "Hey buddy, I've got some property in East St. Louis that I know you'll be happy with."

Immediately I knew what he was implying. My rep. didn't. In fact she asked, "Why would he be trying to sell you property in a grocery store?" I then explained to her very straightforward. I said, "We're in an all White town, I'm probably the only Black they've seen in awhile. I've noticed a certain store clerk has been spying on us to see if I'm going to steal anything." I then pointed her to that clerk who was pretending to be dusting a can of peas. Then here comes the realtor again, "Hey buddy, you'd really like this property I have in East St. Louis." I politely said "I'm good thanks brother." His tone abruptly changed and said, "I'm not your brother, but I've got some really nice property in East St. Louis that I'd love for you to see."

It was at this moment that I told her, "Why don't you go check another section then we can meet at the customer service booth." Mentally, I had slipped back to my Glenville days (The Reinvention of OJ Smith). You must read my autobiography to understand. I knew a public altercation would get me arrested and that probably would have satisfied everyone in the store. I also knew if I am somewhere alone in the store he'd find me and again extend me the property offer. I knew I would punch him in the face and no one would see it. Then we would quickly exit the store and it would be minutes before anyone realized what happened except for the guy cleaning the can of peas. I believe my rep. also knew I had snapped. She then said immediately, "No, lets get out of here. I'm starting to feel uncomfortable too. I'm sorry for bringing you into this environment." She had noticed the clerk following us around. She had begun to get annoyed with the East STL realtor and she felt a lot of the same stares that I felt with all eyes on us.

I didn't know how to feel after that call. I just remembered feeling every time I reflect on being in Corporate America, looking the part, climbing the corporate ladder, effectively managing and leading my team I would be quickly reminded that I'm also Black in Corporate America. I've experienced those subtle reminders at all levels. Whether I'm a manager, supervisor, sales rep. or even director - those reminders seem to find me.

Companies, I just ask you to realize this stuff really happens.

Another experience I had which almost made me think this was going to be normal happened early in my career. You may ask why so many different experiences? These are my experiences. Someone else may have even more than me. Someone may have experienced worse than me. I was a sales representative right out of college. Suit, tie and wing-tipped shoes to work every day. At this point I believed my attire would make people accept me. I believed my White shirts would reduce the purse clutching. I believed my infectious approach and my smile would put people at ease. I somehow believed I just might not cross paths with an extremist. I'm calling this next section:

The Confederate Flag "I will never buy"

At this point I was just working to do a good job. I wasn't even looking for a promotion yet. I wanted to be well received by my customers, by my company and by my supervisors. I recall having the basic objectives in place for every store to assure our full product line was in distribution - to have a display up and to sell a display for the upcoming months. I recall my approach was realizing if they don't know me they're not going to buy from me. I didn't want to be like all the other sales reps. I didn't want to sell them the first time I met them. I wanted to win them over with my service and consistent visibility in their store then I would sell them. This way they came to know me. There was some trust established and I had differentiated myself from all the other reps.

At this point I had been calling on this particular store for several months, which means he had seen me four to five times without me trying to sell him anything. As I completed my service call I asked him for a few minutes to hear my presentation.

It was around 3 or 4 p.m. mid-week. He invited me into his office, which overlooked the entire store. As I walked in there, there was probably the biggest confederate flag I had seen close up. It was displayed at his back as I faced his desk. He sat in his chair facing me. I had a big smile on my face thinking I'm gonna just move forward with my presentation as normal. Then he said "First of all I want you to know I'm never gonna buy a display from you so I don't want you coming in here trying to sell me." I then asked, "Why"? He authoritatively said, "Because you're a nigger." I still had a smile on my face. I didn't want to show him that bothered me. He then continued, "I will let you come into my store and cut in your facings. I don't want you to bring your boss in trying to get a display. I want you to be clear that's never happening. Are we clear?" I said "clear" and that concluded our meeting.

I continued to call on his store for about a year and he held true to his word. He never bought a display from me. He would let me cut in new items and occasionally increase facings on the shelf. Even after I had switched companies and was now working for Hershey's. I recall when I once walked into the store with a boss who asked, "Are we going to sell him a display?" I said, "This store will not buy a display from me." My boss asked why and I said because I'm Black. "Well did he say that?" asked my boss. I briefly explained my encounter in the manager's office. My boss then said something like why do you continue to call on him? I said, "We have 100% distribution and multiple facings on our key items. I'd say we are winning in this store. Just minus the floor display." I was never pressured by the company to sell a display into that store.

I really hoped my boss saw this as a valuable trait. This is adaptability at its best. I could have shared reasons why I didn't feel comfortable going there but I still managed to find a way to make the company profitable in that store, in spite of the environment.

That's what we do. We Blacks in Corporate America. We find ways around the many racial obstacles to keep us in the game; to keep us competitive. To keep us climbing up the corporate ladder.

This reminds me of the fear analogy I used in my previous book. *The Reinvention of OJ Smith.* In my assessments of my 3 fights, I described how my definition of fear may be different from yours simply because of my background.

"I remember while working in corporate America when sales numbers were coming in below our objective. My peers and subordinates would constantly ask, how can you be so calm at a time like this? I'm so afraid. What if we don't make our numbers." I remember that's when I would think of these three incidents. I remember once saying, "I'm calm because I describe fear differently." No one understood what I meant but I clearly recalled my true fears in life.

Excerpt From

The Reinvention of OJ Smith - From Ghetto Streets to

Corporate America

OJ Smith

https://books.apple.com/us/book/reinvention-oj-smith-from-ghetto-streets-to-corporate/id1502092124

This material is protected by copyright.

WHY ME?

I recall once hosting job interviews at a particular hotel chain in Dallas Texas.

I was considered a regular at this hotel because I would host monthly meetings there.

The management team was always happy to see me.

During this particular time they were undergoing some upscale renovations. They were going to be transitioning all hotels to match this particular hotel, which was considered a prototype. With all this being done the hotel owner was in town for a visit. The manager really wanted him to meet me. He wanted to introduce the owner to one of the brand's most loyal and frequent customers. The manager then brought the owner to the room I was interviewing in and introduced me as one of their top customers. He really talked about my loyalty and frequent usage of their property. While it should not matter I need to point out the candidate I was interviewing was a White male.

As he introduced me the owner then stuck out his hand, shaking the hand of the White candidate and thanked him for his loyalty and support. We were all stunned and neither of us corrected him.

Left Out Of Plans...The Market Tour

Clint's company was having a market tour done in the city he lived in. Market tour is when the leaders of the company spend time in a specific market in an effort to assess their presence and performance within that market. This was a big deal because this always involved the CEO, CFO, CPO, COO and other top SVP's within the organization. This gives the local market exposure to Senior Leadership. Previous to the market tour, Clint had been given a specific assignment that would have had him in another market on this particular day. The market tour was in Ohio. His specific assignment was in Boston. I'm calling this portion LOOP.

It had been stressed to Clint the significance of his specific assignment by his direct supervisor. This assignment was to occur Wednesday thru

Friday. Clint had made his travel plans and had discussed with his supervisor what the game plan and approach for this assignment. On Monday of the week of the market tour Clint got an email notification that the tour will be taking place on Thursday and Friday of that week. Clint went to his supervisor and asked should the special assignment be rescheduled now that the market tour was on the new schedule? His supervisor said, "No, you should be done Thursday and able to join the market tour on Friday. You can catch an early flight and join us for lunch."

Clint locked onto that as the game plan for the week. This would make the week less stressful because his boss had helped him prioritize the week's activities. On the Wednesday of the week of the market tour Clint gets a call from his supervisor asking why he was not at dinner on Wednesday to meet the leadership team. Dazed and confused Clint responded, "If you recall, I'm in Boston for the special assignment. I asked you where should I be and you said for me to come here then fly to Ohio to meet up with the tour for lunch on Friday." His supervisor responded, "Well, I would just think you would find it extremely important and opportunistic to be in front of the company's CEO, CFO, CPO and COO. Everyone asked about you at dinner and I didn't know what to tell them." Clint was stunned into silence. His supervisor then said, "You do whatever you feel is necessary and what do you want me to tell them the next time they ask for you?" Clint softly responded, "I will be there in time for lunch on Friday. Where's lunch gonna be?" Abruptly, his supervisor said, "Follow up with one of your peers who's here to get those details."

Clint recalled once when something similar occurred involving one of his White peers, the company, and this same supervisor who had made arrangements for that peer to be transported via the corporate jet so that she wouldn't miss anything. Clint recalled when they asked where she was at dinner, that very same supervisor acknowledged her absence saying something like "She's working on a special assignment, she's multi-tasking."

Clint recalled shortly afterwards she was promoted to a director level. Clint recalled having the conversation with his supervisor before his market tour and thinking, "Wow, they're really looking out for me." Clint never imagined the same wouldn't apply for him. This turned out to be one of the worst weeks in his 30-year career.

Companies, this one is easy in my opinion. Do the same for everyone. In this case Clint wasn't even looking for the corporate jet. He wasn't even looking to be martyred like his White peer. He wasn't expecting a promotion immediately afterwards. All he wanted was the same support she got when she was in the exact same situation.

Clint and I have said Skip is as sharp as our SVP's. Similar to me Skip is well-thought of by subordinates to customers, and internally. The problem is internally there are blockages in his career path. Skip, like both Clint and I, is of high integrity. This next portion is called

THE HARASSING

Skip once received a phone call from one of his subordinates asking him a "what if" question. It went something like this, "What would you do if a female employee that you knew was a good worker wanted to resign over sexual advances from her boss?"

Skip responded, "Are you telling me this is actually happening? At my level I would need to report this immediately." He then said, "Even you at your level if someone has confided this in you it's such a serious situation that it must be reported. I'd tell her to go to HR."

The subordinate then responded, "She has and nothing was done." Skip replied, "Then she should go to her director" (her boss' boss). "She's done that and he said to her that if he has to come there and deal with that the outcome won't be pretty. Now she's afraid to say anything to anyone."

Skip then immediately said, "Because of the level of severity I've got a corporate responsibility to take this to HR and have them look into it. You can help by letting me know who the lady is. If not they're gonna start with you until they find out so they can effectively deal with the situation." The subordinate revealed the victim. Skip then called corporate HR and laid out the allegations as he heard them. He even acknowledged he can't confirm any of this but he trusts the credibility of his subordinate.

HR got involved and Skip felt he had done all he could and what he was supposed to do. A couple days later Skip got a call from HR thanking him for that lead and that they were handling it. The same day Skip was in the presence of his boss, an SVP, who said to him, "That's a pretty bold move you made." Skip asked, "What do you mean?" "You're snitching on VP's now?"

This left Skip stunned. He was thinking he had done the right thing. The admirable thing. He felt handling something like this in the manner he did would be a favorable thing for him. This could be a specific answer to an interview question asked. He was not expecting that response from his supervisor. Personally he thought being called a snitch in the line of business was way out of line. Regardless of it all he knew he had done the right thing. There's no time, place or tolerance for sexual harassment. Remember the "Me Too" movement. This is no different. Only thing is it happened prior to that movement's popularity.

The **Me Too** (or **#MeToo) movement**, is a movement against sexual harassment and sexual abuse where people publicize allegations of sex crimes committed by powerful and/or prominent men. The phrase "Me Too" was initially used in this context on social media in 2006, on MySpace, by sexual harassment survivor and activist Tarana Burke.

Skip's subordinates felt his integrity was demonstrated. That female employee was extremely happy by his efforts. As a result one HR manger got fired. Her supervisor, a district manager, was fired. A VP was demoted because it happened in his team and he didn't act appropriate as company leader. That VP would eventually come back and become Skip's boss. Imagine how awkward.

Once Skip, Clint and I were talking and realized how out of control drinking on the job is. I think that companies should pay closer attention to this. Let's look at a national meeting setting. There's generally a cocktail reception each and every night prior to and after dinner. Danger! Danger! Danger! Simply because we don't know anyone's drinking history or drinking capacity. Some people can't hold their liquor and some don't know when enough is enough. To add to this let's add in a new person with the company attending the meeting. We don't know if that person has been battling alcoholism and we bring them to this meeting with all the alcohol they can drink for free, and approved by the company. Danger! Danger! Danger! The next portion of this book is called

The Drunkenly

Once while attending a company-sponsored event that included customers, Clint witnessed the unbelievable. This was a college football bowl game. Often times Companies would host the KDM's of their top customers at special events such as this. This would be Clint's first attendance at such an event on this level. On the first night, Clint meets his customers in the lobby after the entire group had finished a large group dinner.

There were social groups comprising customers, their representatives and a leader from the company. There was a co-worker of Clint's who had too much to drink. She was very pretty and way out of control. She wore a revealing wrap dress even though her customers were present. Two males who were present were also drinking but were well in control of their consumption. She was very attractive and very flirty. She went into another area that was separated by a door. The two customers followed her. Clint followed her on the advice of his customers who said something like "that is not a good look, you should make sure she's ok." Of course Clint is the only Black of this 50 to 75 person group.

As Clint enters the other room he noticed there's a pool table and the three were playing a game of exotic billiards. There was a lot of inappropriate touching and strong suggestive sexual behavior. Even though Clint was the rookie at this event he knew this had gotten out of hand. Immediately he went and got a manager above him and said something like "I don't know her and I don't know her customers but this doesn't look good." The tenured manager witnessed for himself and agreed. He then told Clint, "I know her and the customers, I'll see to this ending properly." Clint then left and went to his room.

A few weeks after this event Clint got a phone call from an SVP asking him about this incident. Clint explained everything he saw and what he did. The SVP told Clint that next time he needs to handle this better. He should have told her immediate supervisor who was also there. Clint responded, "I didn't know who that was so I got the highest ranking person I saw." He was told something like if you want to see yourself invited to future events like this you need to know who's who. Not just your two or three customers.

Companies, would this have been the disposition if Clint was White? What happened to the manager he did tell? What did Clint do wrong? Here now are two examples of a Black manager doing what is morally right yet being penalized for it.

Skip was called a snitch and now Clint needs to know everyone besides just his customers. Corporate drinking. Danger! Danger! Danger!

Let's look at another example of corporate drinking. This time during a managers meeting with Skip and his company. The meeting was a divisional-level meeting so the attendance was nearly 150 managers of various levels. The meeting was held in Chicago. Once again having pre-dinner and post-dinner cocktails was the norm.

Just think about it. Pre-dinner cocktails, drinks during dinner, and post-dinner cocktails.

Danger! Danger! Danger!

On this particular night it was after dinner. The group had returned to the hotel and several people had gathered for after-dinner cocktails. Skip was sitting with two managers below his level. They were having a simple conversation and each was sipping a beer. Nothing out of hand until she came over to the table. She was another director; one of Skip's peers. She was drunk, speech slurring, stumbling to walk and very loud. She stumbled her way to Skip's table needing help to prevent her from falling. She was an obvious alcoholic. Several within the company new it and seeing her get this drunk was beginning to become a regular occurrence at meetings.

When she stumbled over to Clint's table she fell on his shoulder. That only prompted her to start making inappropriate provocative comments. This made everyone uncomfortable. As she came over she spilled her drink then asked for another. Skip signaled to the bartender to cut her off. That turned into a scene until she eventually got another drink, leaning on Skip and making strong provocative comments. Finally, Skip suggested, "I think it's time to turn in." He had asked one of the female managers to help him escort her to her room. Skip did not want to be alone with her. Drunk or not, Skip, Clint and I had often talked about never being in a situation where we are alone with a White woman while being Black in Corporate America. This situation was almost making that thought inevitable.

Now the managers all decided to leave. Even the female didn't want to be part of this brewing situation. This left Skip where he didn't want to be. One-on-One with a drunken White female at a business meeting. He felt obligated to make sure she got to her room safely. After all, she was his working peer. Skip recalls this as the most uncomfortable he's ever felt in his professional career. The journey through the hotel with her stumbling part of the way and leaning on him. Imagine what this could have looked like.

They get into the elevator and she drunkenly asked, "Are you gonna tuck me in?" Skip didn't even respond to that. The elevator door opened. Her room was probably 10 doors from the elevator. Skip never left the elevator as he watched her stumble to her room, insert the room key and enter her room. The next morning Skip shared with his boss, an SVP, and who was facilitating the meeting. As far as Skip was concerned it was all behind him.

The following week Skip got a call from his boss who was really upset and disappointed over this situation. He blamed Skip for not handling this better. Skip was shocked at how could he be the one at fault over this. Apparently, after she entered her room she exited again and went back downstairs to the lounge for more drinks. This time the CEO was there and witnessed her condition. The CEO then came down hard on the SVP and he decided to blame Skip for not properly handling the situation. The boss felt like Skip should have taken her to her room and assured she stayed there. Think about that. Just like Clint and the college football event. Again, how are the only Black guys at the meeting the ones getting blamed for the bad behavior of others? Especially, when we all feel corporate drinking is Danger! Danger! Danger!

Skip quickly and diplomatically defended himself. He made three valid points:

1) There's no way a Black man taking a drunk White woman to her room can come out of this with a positive outcome.

2) The company including the SVP is well aware of her drinking problems long before this night and this incident.

3) Corporate drinking is Danger! Danger! Danger! Because some can't handle their liquor. Some are even alcoholics and as a company we are enabling their drinking habits. Even an alcoholic on the streets has to come up with the money to get his liquor and we give it to them for free and it's unlimited.

End of the year this was still put into Skip's performance evaluation. Judgment and Problem Solving Skip was rated Needs Improvement citing this specific example.

CHAPTER 9

Overcoming the Challenges African Americans are Facing in the Workplace

Companies this portion of the book is dedicated to you. I feel these are those things a lot of African Americans can easily relate to whenever talking about being Black in Corporate America. In my opinion, if every company had a specific person designated to assess and assure there's is good alignment in these areas you could easily become a better place to work for your minorities. More importantly for all your employees. There would be no repercussions to anyone.

These are simple, non-scientific and very practical areas to focus on. These things would take me 2 minutes to determine how you're company is scoring in these areas. It will require some steps and focuses, mentioned in the previous chapters, to resolve so you may see me referencing back to the earlier chapters.

Let's refer back to chapter 5 and the 8 IFs.

Let's look at all employees. Blacks, Whites, Asians, Indian and Hispanic, men, women, young or old.

Companies, IF you can deliver on those "IFs" consistently with EVERY employee I'm willing to bet you'd have a top place of employment not only for African Americans but for every employee. The key is, you can't deliver on the IFs for some employees and not everyone.

I think the fastest thing for African Americans in the workplace to easily detect is the following:

1) There are two sets of rules.

Of all the Blacks I've spoken with who work in Corporate America and especially Skip, Clint and I, this is the main issue. It often appears what works for others doesn't always work for us. What others get away with we get heavily penalized for. What others get approved for we get denied and rejected. Our work has to be proofed and double proofed whereas with others, once submitted it's good to go. We are not as trusted even if we have a high quality performance record. A friend of mine said he was once given the responsibilities to hire, train and lead his sales team. He was promoted into a position of leadership. The problem was he wasn't given the ability to make the decisions as his peers were. He was never given the opportunity to pick his team. Sounds like accountability without the authority to succeed. It usually will take us longer to get promoted. The Late Dr. Martin Luther King, Jr., once said "we're the last hired and first fired." Being the first fired simply means others can get away with so much more and sometimes even get a promotion out of what we've been fired for.

Two sets of rules. I recall Clint once being called by HR because he had tipped a waitress 22%. According to HR, standard expendable gratuity was 15%. As we all know sometimes we tip our servers 20%. We're not talking a lot of money. Actually we're talking about being Black in Corporate America. The total bill was $59.25. Clint tipped $13.04 for what he thought was outstanding service. He was told by HR that he should have only tipped as much as $8.89 to $11.85. He was asked to pay the difference of $4.15. So that's what it all comes down to. A call from HR to a manager to pay $4.15. Clint was well aware others have tipped more than 15% and even as much as 25-30% and have never been questioned.

Once Clint was with another manager who picked up the lunch tab and tipped the server 25% because the service was outstanding. Clint asked, "Aren't you concerned about HR calling you out on a 25% tip?" He laughed saying, "That would never happen. I've tipped 15, 20 or 25% for nearly my 25 years and have never been questioned over it." Two Sets of Rules.

Skip once hosted a managers meeting in Houston TX. This was a centrally selected location that none of his peers lived in but he stepped up and took the lead on hosting the meeting even though he didn't live there. Nearly 200 people attended this meeting via a rotating 20 per half a day session. There were nearly 20-30 Senior Leaders attending for the entire week. At the conclusion of the meeting, all the Senior Leaders wanted their binders and meeting materials shipped to them so they didn't have to carry it for their travel. Skip efficiently handled it with the hotel and had everything shipped appropriately. This practice was customary after meetings. Two months later Skip gets a call from HR and his supervisor demanding an explanation to the shipping cost. His integrity was challenged.

Skip reminded his supervisor of the meeting and everyone's request to have their material sent to them. His supervisor (while in the presence of HR) said, "You should have not offered to do this." Skip said, "but this is what we do after meetings. This isn't the first time we've done this." He wasn't supported by his supervisor. He was reprimanded and written up by HR. Later that year during his performance evaluation he received an overall average rating but was rated below average in the area of "Judgement and Decision Making." The next similar meeting that occurred Skip watched the hosting manager do the same thing along with the approval of the same supervisor. Two Sets of Rules.

Clint was at a national meeting and on this particular night each manager was to host their own specific team dinner. This meeting was held in Orlando Florida. Each employee was given a $25 gift card for dinner that evening but many saw this as an opportunity to eat at a fairly decent restaurant. The main objective was that they ate with their respective teams. A fairly decent restaurant would extend the per person cost to $37. Because Clint's team wanted to eat at this particular restaurant Clint decided to host the dinner and personally pay the difference of $12 per person.

As they arrived at the restaurant Clint quickly noticed five to six other company teams were there also. He walked over to one of the managers asking, "With our $25 cap how are you going to handle the $12 difference." One manager said, "I'm letting them keep their cards and I'm paying for the dinner. You're at a national meeting. You'll be fine."

Clint realized this was a tenured manager and knew he probably couldn't get away with that. He then went to another manager asking the same question. This manager said, "I'll apply their cards to the total, then I'll expense the balance. That's what my VP told me to do." Wow, Clint thought. Two totally different approaches and none were with the integrity he was planning to display. Remember, Clint was going to personally pay the difference himself. Clint wasn't going to expense it and certainly not put the entire tab on the company. He then saw another of his peers. This one had the same direct supervisor as Clint. He asked her the same question and she said, "Don't be so uptight, relax. The goal of this dinner is that it's a team dinner. All you're doing is having dinner. I'm going to expense the drinks and appetizers and their $25 cards will pay for dinner."

Now Clint has three different perspectives on how to handle dinner. He felt if he asked a fourth person he'd get even a different perspective from the first three. About a month after the meeting Clint was called by his supervisor who was questioning his dinner plans for that particular night. The manager asked, "With 14 team members your dinner total should have been $350 or less. Why is it more?" Clint proudly explained, "We had three home office people join us for dinner." Since it was team night the home office people were asked to join with various teams in an effort enhance internal working relationships. Clint further explained, "Each of them had their own $25 cards. I explained to my team to order and whatever exceeded our $25x14 budget I was going to personally pay for myself. I explained this was my appreciated gesture for all their working efforts and helping us deliver strong to date business results." His explanation seemed to satisfy but he thought, "Wow, I wonder what will happen to those other three managers.

Clint was so glad he had not followed the advice of the other managers. He went to each of them asking how they dealt with the "heavy eyes" that were on the expense reports covering the dinner that night. The most hurtful thing was their responses. Each one of them referenced they had not been questioned. No one asked them anything about that night. Clint played by the book. Personally paid the difference and was questioned. The other three managers exceeded the allotted $25 budget in various ways. None of them were ever questioned.

Two Sets of Rules. Clint could only imagine if he had followed their advice what would have happened to him.

I recall once taking my daughter to school. There was a new waiver that was to be signed that I didn't agree with. As we walked into the front door we were told we were not gonna be able to get her locker and computer. Basically we turned around and left. Later that night I decided to go on and sign the waiver, mainly for my daughter's sake. I was gonna come in within the next couple of days to do the signing. The next day I received messages asking when am I coming in to sign the agreement. The problem was the fact that there were many other families that had not signed the agreement. Not one of them had their child turned around at the door and refused to get their locker assignment. Not one of the other families were pressed to get the waiver signed. This I know, so I ask why me? Two Sets of Rules.

Companies, the main point here is it cannot be obvious to African Americans that there are two sets of rules. In each of these examples and many others out there it's very obvious that the same rules are not applying to everyone.

The next opportunity area for most companies is that of

2) Ineffective Onboarding

Many African Americans even the ones who excel and do extremely well climbing the corporate ladder will often admit the lack of a mentor or ineffective onboarding. They figured a lot out for themselves. They were with a good company and as long as their performance met the gold standard they were good. Other African Americans in the workforce may not be as fortunate. There are many who could have done much better with a trustworthy mentor or an effective onboarding program. They could have possibly climbed higher on the corporate ladder. Think of sports. The kid in whom the coaches invest time will likely do better than the kid in whom no time is invested.

I wrote in my autobiography *The Reinvention of OJ Smith, From Ghetto Streets to Corporate America* of how I missed having a father figure. That was a form of mentorship for me growing up that I didn't have. As well as I've done for myself in life I will always feel with good manly guidance I could have done better. In my book I wrote:

"I had recalled a conversation I had with a VP where he asked, "Who was my mentor"? I said, "I don't have one and have never really had one." I had gone through life imagining what to do, never knowing for sure if I was on the right path but trying to be successful. He then said, "I think you've done quite well for yourself. Not having a mentor, you've navigated yourself into a Director level position and you're well thought of within the industry and the company." I think that was one of the most powerful things ever said to me. I'd remembered making the baseball team as a kid when I didn't't even know how to put the glove on my hand. Likewise, I made the team without having a mentor."

Excerpt From

The Reinvention of OJ Smith - From Ghetto Streets to Corporate America

The value of good mentoring and effective onboarding plays a significant role for every employee but especially for African Americans. Remember one of the 8 IF's.

'IF, they had an effective mentor within the company helping them with their career path.'

Some companies do this well and others don't. Sometimes this is structured. Other times that VP will constantly follow up and invest good guidance with a subordinate they met at a national meeting. That's good also but unfortunately many African Americans are not handpicked. I personally believe everyone in the company should have a mentor. Think of Clint, at the meeting and the $25 dinner budget. A good mentor would have been helpful. It sounds to me as if the one peer he went to who said their VP told them... had some sort of mentor support. Perhaps the reason his other peers felt so confident to handle the dinner expenses that evening was because they had some trusted confidant that had previously shared with them some of the minor do's and don'ts. Clint didn't have this.

However it's done I think this is a vital ingredient. Whether you assign a mentor to your employees. Whether you ask them who they want as their mentor or just continually follow up and see that they are in a comfortable mentoring relationship. I think it's also important to challenge leadership to assure they are mentoring someone.

This is important because if you've hired future leaders, that means they're aspiring to eventually be in the roles of your current leaders.

What goes along with effective mentoring is inclusion.

3) Inclusion is slightly different from mentoring because peers can play an important role here. Peers have the opportunity to ensure that any new employee is always included. Think back to Skip, when he was new in his role. He was never really included by his peers. They'd leave when he joined them at the lunch table. Then the ultimate display of non-inclusion was when the group (managers and peers) secretly met

afterwards to go out without him. This is hurtful no matter who you are but if you're the only African American it is extremely hurtful. You began to think what if they agree on a new start time for the meeting, how would you know? What if they all decide no questions and the meeting will end early, then you show up asking lots of questions. What if they're talking about the Black guy. Race may not have played a role in why they didn't include Skip but whenever we're not included the first thing we do is wonder why. Perhaps we look in the mirror to see what's different about us from the rest. If there had been several other Blacks Skip wouldn't feel he was not included due to race. But when you're the only Black and you're not included, that's the first thing that comes to mind.

I think the final area of challenge for many African Americans is:

4) Racial Identity. Sometimes we're our own worst enemy. Sometimes some of us are not comfortable being us. I love being Black. I love Black people. I love and enjoy being around all people. I prefer fun and joyful people over anyone else. I believe there's good and bad in all of us. I don't believe all White people are the enemy. Likewise, I don't believe all Black people are bad. There are some White people that are truly the enemy to Blacks and there are definitely some bad Black people. I love the various shades of Black people. I'm always happy and proud to see us as a people prosper and do well.

When I watch the TV game show 'The Price is Right' I get excited for the winners as they show their excitement. I love seeing the Black person win. Equally, I love seeing all the winners Whites, Black, Asian, Indian, Latino, male, female, young or old. It doesn't matter if I've experienced that feeling and know how it feels. Happiness has no color. I don't, and have never, apologized for being Black. Growing up when I was introduced to the Black athletes, superheroes or entertainers I quickly relished in their Blackness. I've even thought to myself if they can make it then there's hope for me. Even as a youngster with my superheroes as Batman and Superman I glorified the Blackness of John Stewart's Green Lantern. Then you also have DC's Cyborg and Marvel's Falcon and War Machine. Mace Windu whose powers were the closest to Yoda in the Star Wars saga.

I often think about the dude in the stairwell of corporate office where he was afraid to speak in public but when it was just us one–on–one he opened up and carried on a conversation like we were long lost friends. I think of Blacks who have made it up the corporate ladder without a mentor but then also without mentoring others. I think of the Blacks who are slow to come and welcome the new Black into the organization. I think of the Blacks who would have changed the radio station when their manager told them. What's even worse are the ones who would have already had the station set onto a White radio station as a way to impress their White supervisor. It's as if they are trying to say, "Hey look at me, I like White music too."

Thanks to my years in Corporate America I've been able to live in the best neighborhoods, unlike when I was growing up in Cleveland. I've always lived in very nice neighborhoods where unfortunately there were little to no other Black families. Several times I was the only Black in the neighborhood. As much as I enjoyed living in a nice neighborhood I really hated being the only Black. I recall moving into an affluent neighborhood in St. Louis. We lived there for two years. Across the street from us was another Black family. Outside of the two of us the rest of the neighborhood was all White. That Black family never ever spoke to us. Not once, not privately, not ever. I recall even once going over to introduce myself one summer day while they were outside. The guy and who I assumed was his wife never even looked up at me. I knew this wasn't their demeanor overall because I'd see them hanging with the White neighbors. They would often go out of their way to speak to them as they drove up and down the streets. It was as if they wanted to be the only Blacks in the neighborhood and when we moved in we spoiled it for them.

I grew up in the ghetto. An all-Black neighborhood in Cleveland Ohio. I recall when the hustler dudes fell into some money they'd go out and get a White girl as if that would elevate their status. I often wondered, "Why not get a girl from the neighborhood?" Then when the money was gone they'd no longer have the White girl.

I recall once talking to a Black dude who said he only dates White girls. I asked, "Why?" He said, "because I can see the finer things in life through her." I thought to myself, that's the most shallow reason I've ever heard. I would date whomever I was attracted to. I've dated Whites, Asian and Latino before. I would never racially select anyone. I want someone who's mentally in sync with me. We enjoy the same things. We want the same things out of life. We enjoy each other's company. My wife of 34 years happens to be Black. I'm with her simply because of the reasons I just mentioned and not because she's Black.

I often think of the slavery days. When the slave catchers used Blacks to capture Blacks. How much the Black slave catcher wanted to impress his White massa. I often think of the little Black girls who don't want to play with their Black baby dolls, they only want to play with the White dolls. I think of the small private predominantly White high schools. When it's prom or homecoming time within the entire school of 1,000 there's seven Black boys and six Black girls. Each of the Black boys decide to take a White girl to the prom or homecoming without ever even asking the Black girls first. I always wonder how that makes the Black girl feel. I know of a scenario where it played out like this and of the six Black girls four went to prom together as a group of girls. One decided not to attend prom at all. One decided to attend prom with a White male friend.

I recall the time (Chapter 4) when I was at the national meeting and it was breakfast time. I was comfortable eating with my two Black friends. They were comfortable eating with me, even if this meant a table of Blacks within a sea of White employees. The natural reaction was to split up and separate ourselves but we didn't and I'm glad we didn't. There are two songs that constantly play in my head, "Whatcha See is Whatcha Get" 1971 by the Dramatics. If you see me, you see I'm Black and that's what you're gonna get. I'm not gonna try to be anything or anyone else. The other song is 'Say It Loud, I'm Black and I'm Proud" 1968 by James Brown. This song is very self-explanatory. However, I place my emphasis on "Loud, Black and Proud."

I asked another good friend of mine to read excerpts from this book. I wanted his perspective since he is currently in Corporate America. Here's what he shared.

"Also, the negative perception of Blacks in management is supporting each other. One job I had the Director a republican btw (by the way) hired half his senior management who were Black. About once a quarter or semi-annually we would come together for an hour, brothers/sisters lunch to bond and uplift each other. Of course others complained and said we were being exclusive even though they were free to join, we met openly, and when they gathered together it was called strategy sessions. Our meetings were viewed as a coup de tat even though the Director was White and we all loved and respected him and were loyal to his leadership."

In my opinion, there has to come a time when seeing more than one Black person together no longer poses a threat.

CHAPTER 10

Realize what's Racist and what's Prejudice

I am no Doctor, Professor, Theologian or expert. I don't even profess to be. I'm just a guy sharing my perspective. For this section I've gathered perspectives from more than 50 people to help me share this content.

Racism is defined by the dictionary as a belief or doctrine that has inherent differences among the various human racial groups determine cultural or individual achievement, usually involving the idea that one's own race is superior and has the right to dominate others or that a particular racial group is inferior to others. Racism by dictionary definition is a policy, system of government, etc., based upon or fostering such a doctrine; discrimination. Racism defined is a hatred or intolerance of another race or other races. I don't believe most companies are racist. The problem is the thin lines. The synonyms of racism like bias. Bigotry. Discrimination. Unfairness. Two sets of rules. These are highly probable in most companies.

The dictionary defines Prejudice as an unfavorable opinion or felling formed beforehand or without knowledge, thought, or reason. Prejudice defined is any preconceived opinion or feeling, either favorable or unfavorable. Prejudice defined is unreasonable feelings, opinions, or attitudes, especially of a hostile nature, regarding an ethnic, racial, social or religious group. Unfortunately I do believe many companies have prejudice practices.

More so, I believe many companies have people and many in key positions that practice these prejudgment behaviors. Some subconscious and some intentional.

Let's look at some synonyms that connect prejudice and racism – Bigotry, Bias, Discrimination. This is often seen in the workplace. There are even examples with Clint, Skip and my stories in the previous chapters. Let's look at some other synonyms to the word prejudice like ageism, sexism, injustice, preconceptions, chauvinism, partiality, unfairness and narrow mindedness. Unfortunately these are areas that come up within the workforce. Ageism, have you ever experienced or felt like once you hit a certain age and your company no longer values your performance? Or were even trying to steer you out of the organization? Sexism - women have you ever suspected you were being paid less for the same job a male counterpart was doing? Unfairness - I think of Skip and the example of the meeting expense report. Especially, when the same didn't apply to his peers. I think about Clint with the Orlando national meeting and the $25 dinner expense.

I talked with several Whites and Blacks and asked them sincerely about their feelings on race relations. There seems to be a big gap in how some Whites feel versus how some Blacks feel about the other race. There are some Whites that feel when they are in the presence of Blacks they're in danger. Ironically, there are some Whites that feel if danger comes upon them and they are with a Black friend, the Black friend will be able to handle it. They feel the Black is used to this kind of stuff and will know how to get us out of this. Perhaps that's why we see a lot of purse clutching and car doors locking when we're in the vicinity. Many Blacks feel Whites simply don't like them. Many Blacks feel Whites talk about them outside of their presence. Whites are less likely to say that Blacks are treated less fairly than Whites. Whites are more likely to say they don't feel there's much racial hostility towards Blacks in the country. There are some Whites who only see the Black Lives Matter movement as an aggressive act of violence from Blacks whenever a

Black has been slain at the hands of a White. Remember, Black Lives Matter was designed as an online community to help combat anti-Black racism across the globe. There are many Whites that feel Black on Black crime is a bigger issue than Whites on Black crime in America.

Many Blacks are highly skeptical that the country will make the necessary changes for Blacks to achieve equal rights to Whites. Many Blacks feel the actions by companies as a result of the George Floyd killing will be short-lived and quickly forgotten.

Think back in the previous chapter where Clint was asked to present to the Senior Leadership team and then it was cancelled and to this date has never been mentioned again.

Many Blacks will say they have personally experienced discrimination or been treated unfairly because of their race or ethnicity more than once. What's really startling is even those Blacks who have risen to positions of prominence will say they have had similar experiences along their climb of the corporate ladder. There were several Whites from my sample group who really feel that Blacks are inherently criminals. Many Blacks feel that Whites feel they are smarter. The bottom line here is that Blacks and Whites share very different perspectives when it comes to race relations.

I'm don't believes all Whites are the same. I will again and again clarify some feel...etc. I know of good-hearted Whites who will never fully support the Black Lives Matter movement because they cannot see beyond what they've seen on TV- aggressive protest, looting, rioting, property destruction and graffiti defacing. Many of them don't even know the true intentions of the Movement. Many of them don't recognize or are slow to acknowledge the many Whites that were a part of the Movement and involved in defacing buildings and aggressive protesting. Many of them feel if Blacks when accosted by police would simply comply there would be no problems. Again, these are just different perspectives from us when it comes to race relations.

We often hear in the news where someone uses the "N' word. Perhaps they were a teacher, a coach or a famous TV personality. Just the other day I read a college football team walked out of a team meeting because the coach used the "N" word with emphasis on the "ER." Many Blacks are not surprised. Many Blacks feel this happens all the time. It's only caught a few times and that's usually when the world reacts. Some Whites feel this is as rare as we hear about it and is not happening as often as we think. Different perspectives. During one of the conversations I had with a good White friend of mine he revealed he doesn't believe people are talking like that as much. He then went on to say his Dad uses the word but he's not a racist or a bigot. He'll use the "N" word if a car driven by a Black person cuts him off. He further explained it's not different than had it been a fat person, he would have called them "fatso" or had it been a woman he might have called her "dumb broad." I thought to myself "Hmmmmm."

Different perspectives.

Perhaps three things that irk me the most are in no order - purse clutching, car door locking and being passed up in a service line. The other day I was in a line at the grocery store in the deli section. When I walked up there was a line of two customers that had established. I would be the third person to be serviced. As time went by another lady walked towards the line. While it should not matter, she was a White woman. At this point the person in front of me was being serviced and I was clearly next. Another person came out to assist with the servicing. He walked over to the White lady and said, "May I help you?" This really irked me. Now, I have two issues. (1) Is the fact that he didn't assume I might have been there next? He should have asked "Who's next?" If he had looked at the formation, I was in the line and this lady had just walked up to the glass display and began to wait. What bothered me even more is (2) the fact that she knew I was ahead of her and she went on with her order as if she was entitled to be next. I had to speak out on this. I said to him, "Hey I was clearly next in line." Then I had to say something to her. I said, "Ma'am I was clearly here before you." Then she gave a lame response, "Oh, I thought you were already taken care of. I'm sorry." I wanted to challenge her on that but decided to end it there. This wasn't the first time and won't be the last that this happens.

As irritating as all these acts are, I don't call them racist. I do feel there's a lot of prejudice and bigotry. I also think it's very easy for us to quickly generalize people and say things like "You people" or "all Whites" or "Blacks are..." None of those statements can end in truth because every Black person doesn't think like me and there are many Black perspectives that I differentiate myself from. Companies, it's important not to make similar assumptions in the workplace. But how often does it actually happen? On the humorous side, I recall the movie "Soul Man" with C. Thomas Howell. He tries to pass himself as a Black to enter into a predominantly White college. When all the Whites saw him they quickly began to prejudge and generalize. There's one scene where they were playing a pick up basketball game. Everyone wanted the C. Thomas character on their team because they thought all Blacks were good at basketball. C. Thomas was horrible during the game and it puzzled everyone.

I recall someone said to me something like, "you're a racist" I asked "why" and they responded, "You are a big Cleveland Indians fan. I've seen you wear their jerseys. I've seen you wear the jersey depicting their logo Chief Wahoo. Today, that's been outlawed as offensive to Native Americans so that means you're a racist. Are you gonna get rid of it? Are you gonna burn it?" To me, it's what you do after the gained knowledge. During the times I wore the jersey the whole team and organization wore it. As we explore how such logos personally offend different cultures - and those teams have decided to use a different logo - or in some cases changed their names I personally believe it's how you react once you know how it impacts others. If I were to continuously wear it knowing some find it offensive, and that it's no longer the teams logo, that would make me extremely insensitive In my opinion. This is similar to the friend who owns a confederate flag but keeps it folded because he doesn't want to offend anyone.

Let's take a look at the various generations within the work place.

BABY BOOMERS are born before and until 1963. They are generally described as highly productive workers, hardworking team players and mentors to the younger lot. But there are some baby boomers who are the opposite. Baby Boomers are often perceived as less adaptable, and less collaborative. But there are some baby boomers who are extremely adaptable and collaborative. I'm one.

GEN X. Generation X are those born between 1963 to 1980. They are generally described as sharp in managerial skills. Good in generating revenue and problem solving. But there are some who are the exact opposite. Often times Gen X people are perceived as less cost effective and have less executive presence. Again, there are some who are really outstanding cost effective workers and who have a great executive presence especially when working for an out-of-the-box thinking company.

MILLENNIALS. They are born 1980 to 1995. They are usually described as the most enthusiastic workers. They are usually tech savvy. They usually are perceived as the most entrepreneurial and opportunistic workers. They can sometimes be perceived as lazy and unproductive and self-obsessed.

The bottom line is I believe there are some baby boomers who fit the millennial description and some millennials who fit the Gen X description and some Gen X people who fit the baby boomers description. I believe there are some baby boomers who are a mix of all three descriptions. I believe there are some Gen X people who fit all three descriptions and the same for millennials. My point is you can't generalize because when you do, you leave no opportunity for "out-of-the-box" thinking. With no out-of-the-box thinking you get the "cookie cutter" approach and no "out-of-the-box" activities. Think of the Magic Johnson example. If the above definitions held true, Magic who's a baby boomer would have been considered less adaptable and less collaborative. He was probably the most adaptable in that game. Remember, he played all five positions. He had a game high 42 points. The night before the game he called his Dad and said something like, "I'm gonna put my scoring hat on for the game since our star scorer is out." He was the most collaborative. That is to say he worked best with his other teammates in that game. In fact, that has been his strongest feature throughout his entire career. I believe the reason they won was because the coach did not put him in a box and keep him there. He allowed "out-of-the-box" gameplay and was open-minded to not generalize.

He could have thought, "He's just a rookie, I won't expect him to carry this load tonight."

Companies, can you see yourselves doing something similar?

The next area of concern is what I'm calling

THE GREAT DIVIDE. Often times the issues a lot of African Americans face are with peers and above. Usually, not with subordinates and external customers. Although, issues with subordinates and external customers can occur. I think back to the subordinate of mine who made the POW-MIA comment. I never really recognized him as a problem simply because I was the boss.

Let's look at **SUBORDINATES**. As a manager of a team I believe if you treat them right and deliver on the 8 IF's within your realm of control you're gonna have a good experience. Even if there are some IF's you can't deliver due to corporate mandates they will see you as more "for" them than against them. In some cases they may be your biggest advocates. During a 360 degree internal review the manager gets outstanding reviews from the subordinates. As a manager if you're getting them promoted and providing them with good professional guidance they're going to look beyond your skin color in most cases. Some will even leave even want to come work for the manager when that manger is promoted into a different area or even if the manager leaves the company the subordinate will strongly consider following. The manager that allows the subordinate to think out-of-the-box as long as they're delivering results will be looked upon favorably. When the subordinate sees the manager going "to bat" for them that is when they know the manager is pushing for them even during the midst of corporate opposition. Even if the subordinate sees the manager doing this for someone other than them they believe the manager would do the same for them.

Let's refer back to chapter 5 and the 8 IFs.

Let's look at all employees. Blacks, Whites, Asians, Indian, Hispanic, Men or women, young or old.

If the following were evidently equal for everyone the problem would be solved.

IF, they were paid well for what they do. Sometimes the manager cannot directly control this but they can ensure the employee is getting what they're supposed to get. They can also have an impact on annual merit increases.

IF, they had an effective mentor within the company helping them with their career path. The manager can recommend and sometimes even offer guidance on this one. Often times the subordinate looks at the manager as their mentor.

IF, they found their job or responsibility challenging. The manager can have some impact in this area with autonomy given and with extra responsibility to show trust.

IF, they felt they were fairly and timely promoted.

IF, they constantly felt they were involved in key decision-making.

IF, they were evidently and constantly reminded that they were appreciated and valued. Here's where the manager can really score well. Think of Clint and the $25 dinner night. Clint told his team he was personally picking up the difference to show his appreciation of their efforts.

IF, they were empowered to make decisions to help the company win.

IF, they were sincerely trusted to do their job. These last two can almost go hand-in-hand. They can really go well if the manager both empowers them, shows trust then uses that as an example of above average performance for that subordinate. This can be the ultimate way to show the subordinate you're fighting for their professional success.

Let's look at **EXTERNAL CUSTOMERS**. This one is quite simple. The external companies from my experience have been always more diverse in culture. If you're helping their business grow, you're good with them. There have been some companies that have even called their business partner companies out, for their lack of cultural diversity. Often times it's the external customers that save the African Americans in the workforce. When their own company is slow to promote them it's almost impossible to overlook the relationship and impact they have on their customers.

A TV news reporter can get overlooked for a job numerous times within the organization but if they are constantly winning Emmy Awards for their work done in the field it simply means others recognize their talents and the value they add. If they are becoming a local favorite by viewers it's hard to deny their real impact. I was once told, "Win with your customers and the rest will fall into place. Your business will grow, your career will grow and you will always be well thought of."

Skip once attended a top-to-top meeting with one of his largest customers. A top-to-top meeting is a meeting with the top leaders of two companies in an effort to strategically align business plans for the year or next few years. It can sometimes be referred to as the "never say no" meeting because all of the key decision-makers are present. No one will ever have to say "let me go to my boss and see…" The two companies will meet over a two to three day period to plan strategies from top to bottom that will impact business with mutual benefits. These meetings are usually attended by the CEO's of both the organizations who are actively engaged and involved - both CEO's and their selected staff that have a direct impact on the business. Because it was

Skip's customer he was in attendance with his team of eight. This included the representative that called on the account, manager of the representative, Skip, VP of Sales, VP of Marketing, VP of sales development, CFO and the CEO. All White male except for Skip. For the customer there were nine in attendance including their CEO and VP of purchasing among others. Of the nine, four women, three African Americans, two Latino's and five Whites.

At the conclusion the VP of purchasing made the comment, "I'm concerned when you come to us and want to talk business strategies for our various markets which includes suburban, inner city, Hispanic, Indian and Asian communities. You're a group of all White men. How can you begin to understand the cultural market demands within different markets?"

What more needs to be said? She then added, "Because of Skip's perspective our business has grown. Imagine what it could be if he had a more culturally diverse support team." Everyone was silent. In my opinion he should have immediately been valued by his company. In actuality, they did nothing with that comment and felt the meeting was an overall success.

Let's look at **PEERS**. Problems can exist here because there's sometimes the feeling of competing for the same job. There's a feeling that they should have the position you got. When I became a director I recall having such a conversation with a peer that I had once trained. He bitterly felt it should have been him in the director's role. He went on to say, "Nothing against you, I'm happy for you but I can do that job." I responded with something like, "I too can do this job. I've been with the company 4 years longer than you. Today, we are peers, which means it has taken me longer to get to this level than it has you. Now, that I'm here you want it, instead of me." We never talked again after that.

Peers will sometimes get into direct competition with you once you're in a role simply because they don't want you to pass them up to the next level. They don't want you to get there before them. Some peers can't conceive the possibility of working for you. In some cases they can't see working for an

African American especially if they were in direct competition for the same role. This can often lead to non-inclusion and even a "good ol' boy network." Think back to the previous chapter where Skip was not being included with the other team members. Sometimes this can also lead to what I call "fake inclusion." Fake inclusion is when you're invited into the group but all the focus turns to you. They never talk about what they actually are thinking or their normal topics. They will never discuss, "how tos or shortcuts." They don't want you to know the easy way of getting the assignment done. They will secretly talk about you and whisper and laugh as you approach them. Once you're there they will turn the conversation to a patronizing and obviously insincere chat.

Peers will sometimes damage your reputation by sharing with the manager something about you. I'm not saying all peers are like this. There are some peers who really have your back. They do a great job of helping you acclimatize into your new role. In fact, I believe most peers are good. They will always make sure you know what the shortcuts are. They will keep you current if they feel something important was shared outside of your presence.

Some peers will give you a wake up call to assure you make the meeting on time. They will let you know how the meetings flow. What things the managers like and dislike. They will make sure you know how not to get on the manager's bad side.

Often times within the team you're in, you can have one peer that will help, and another that will let you walk off a cliff. It's been known for peers to spread bad words to customers against their peers. Clint picked up a customer that was once handled by a peer. During the handoff meeting the customer made a comment something like, "Man, I'm sure gonna miss you. Are you sure this rookie will take care of us?" His peer then responded, "I'm just a phone call away." His peer should have entrusted the responsibility to Clint. He should have assured the customer he would be in great hands.

OJ SMITH

He should have had Clint's back on this, instead he suggested when Clint fumbles just call me and I'll be there. Perhaps the only good thing from this is that it happened in the open. This happens many times behind the back of the African American. This sort of thing can happen with any employee no matter what the race but it tends to happen too often with African Americans.

This happened to me once and went on for several months until the customer actually told me about it. I can respect and appreciate the fact that my peer and the customer had an excellent and trusting relationship. It just made me think how could this person really have my back when talking to our boss. Think back to the 8 IF's.

IF, they were sincerely trusted to do their job. Not just by management but also by their peers, by their subordinates and by their customers. Certainly there was no trust in this situation.

Now let's look at **SUPERVISORS**. Unfortunately, as good as you can be, if they don't see you as part of their plan, it ain't happening. I'm not talking about people who are sub-par performers and have gone as far as they can. Good management detects that and accurately contributes to the management cadre. They are good at assuring "right people in the right positions" in an unbiased way. They are good at ensuring that the right people are properly trained, qualified and capable of working in positions of organizational leadership.

However, there are those managers, supervisors or even leaders that don't practice these good traits. Think back to the previous chapter where Skip's manager told him his boss said that as long as he was the boss, Skip would never make it to the next level. This without any performance-related issues. The only solid takeaway was this person did not like Skip. Perhaps Skip didn't speak to him once. Perhaps Skip accidentally stepped on his toe without saying excuse me. Maybe he just doesn't like the way Skip dressed, laughed, walked or talked. It's even possible he just didn't like Skip because he was being Black in Corporate America. For 30 of Skip's 30+ years with the company he's received an above average performance rating. So why would that SVP say that?

We've all had that supervisor that has often reminded us that our future is in their hands. A friend told me they were once told by their supervisor "make no mistake, I'm the only friend you've got." I said, "Why would he say that? You're the most outgoing and popular person I know." My friend then further explained, "Of course he didn't mean it literally but what he did mean was behind closed doors when it's time to 'sell me up' into the organization, he was the only highly credible person to do that. Without him selling me up in the organization it's like running for office but having no votes. You could be the best performer but if you got no votes you ain't going nowhere." Here's where you start competing against those who have mentors. Those mentors are behind the closed doors advocating for their mentees. Here's where we Blacks in Corporate America can often lose out. We don't have the support at that level. As I see it, there are two main reasons we don't.

A) We are not on boarded as well as our counterparts. Think back to the chapter on inclusion, onboarding and mentors. We clearly identified that as an area of opportunity.

B) The other reason is, we as Blacks are not visible "behind those closed doors." Just think about it, for both Skip and Clint there are no other Blacks above them. So, who's gonna advocate for them? If their direct manager doesn't then who? If their direct manager does advocate for them but is then told his boss said as long as he's there Skip would never advance, then what? If Clint is chosen to train all the fast-track employees for positions he's clearly capable of, who's advocating for him?

I once recall meeting a Black man who was (in my opinion) the sharpest dude I've ever met in Corporate America. He was one of five divisional presidents for a major Fortune 500 company. He was very down to earth with his Blackness. He was very comfortable being Black in public, unlike the "stairwell hello" dude. I met him at a diversity and inclusion conference. We talked and I asked him about being that high in a predominantly White company. I asked him something like "what was your journey like and how are others pathing to also get there?" I will never forget the three major things he said from that conversation.

1) It has indeed been a struggle. No mentor. No one pulling him up from within the company. He said his strength was his external customers and his subordinates. The company could not deny his talents. He was always the best in those areas. He identified those as areas he could control. What the company did beyond that was out of his control.

2) He made sure he always brought in other Blacks. Talented and good working Blacks. People who wanted to climb the corporate ladder. He said his team was always 10% of good talented African Americans. He recalled the sad thing was he outperformed his peers in this area year after year. He recalled when the Rodney King beating occurred the company displayed a high attentive sensitivity to race relations within the organization. He was used as a model of success. From that point on he always had an internal advocate. His CPO was that KDM shot caller (from the beginning of the book). Every organization needs such a person.

3) He effectively used that leverage to introduce a pipeline for his replacements. He's the highest ranking Black in the company but he has always assured his previous positions were filled by other rising star minorities. As one of five divisional presidents he said they each fly a corporate jet to where they need to be. At the point we were talking he said he was the most tenured divisional president, which meant his voice carried a lot of weight among his peers. He gave me his card and invited me to join his team. He said, "You can get here with us, I'd make sure of it."

CHAPTER 11

PURPOSE

Many times we go to work looking for the wrong things. In my opinion work is a means to an end. We go, provide a service, talent or skill. The company pays us for that. We provide for our family food, clothing and shelter. Purpose is the reason for which something exists or is done. We have the job so that we can get paid. Purpose has an intended or desired result. Payday. There are too many times we go to work and look for more. Some go to work to make friends. Others look for their future spouse. Many look for fuzzy warm feelings. Such a job that delivers all those things is great; but when they don't deliver your next love affair and still paid you for the work you provided, that's where the purpose of that job has been met.

I often have said there's a difference between **THE JOB, THE CAREER and THE DREAM JOB**. They're all good and do their part in terms of providing pay for services rendered.

The JOB is where we don't really like to go. Or perhaps it's a summer job during school breaks. We don't really care for the boss, the people and sometimes not even what we do on the job. We may not even care for the industry we're working in. We simply do it because it pays us each week. It's not necessarily always unskilled labor. There can sometimes be White-collared jobs within this category. The job may sometimes pay well and may often times pay us just enough to get by. This can lead us to sometimes working two jobs.

Let's define motivational fit as whenever the employer is looking to pay big for a certain set of skills. The employee has that certain set of skills, enjoys using the set of skills and is very good at that set of skills. What you are good at doing, what you enjoy doing and what they are looking for is a fit. It's motivationally fitting to both parties. With the job there generally is no motivational fit. It's not motivationally fitting if you can do the job but you don't enjoy doing it. With the job there is usually no job loyalty. Turnover may be higher than other jobs because as soon as something remotely better comes along the employee is quick to jump ship. Remember, the job is not where you go to look for friends. It's a means to an end. It's a way to deliver a service that will monetarily reward you for that service. That monetary reward is your means to provide food, shelter and clothing for your family. With the job, don't expect to be appreciated for what you do. Just do it and get paid. If you are shown appreciation that's great and will feel rewarding but it may not happen as often as you want it or need to hear it. Normally, this job does not allow you to fulfill any of your purpose.

You may or may not get a promotion. If you do, that's awesome. If the company is showing that kind of interest and you're enjoying it, this job may even be more than just THE JOB.

THE CAREER. Here's where you want your ego stroked more. You actually like this job or at least you want to like it. This is the job you selected because of what and how they do business. You may have even studied about doing this in college. It's your expectation to be here awhile so you are looking for friends on the job or certainly within the industry. With this job you certainly hope there's a motivational fit. In this job promotions can lead you to the career path you want. You're extremely proud of your accomplishments. This job can often pay extremely well. Well enough for some people to deal with whatever shortfalls it may have. The pay promises to be good.

I worked in Corporate America for nearly 30 years. It was a career job for me. It was more than just "the job." However, it was not a dream job for me. Don't get me wrong, I enjoyed what I did. I was good at it. At times there was a strong lasting motivational fit. I was considered successful and well thought of by the company. I'm sure there were some who didn't care for me but that's anywhere. I enjoyed going to work everyday. At one point I had 24 years of perfect attendance with the company until recognizing perfect attendance went away when new leadership came.

As I mentioned, as much as I enjoyed my job it was not my **DREAM JOB**. The dream job is what you've wanted to be when you were a little kid. A football player. An actor or actress. A singer in a Grammy winning rock band. I wanted to be a Major League Baseball player. There are some people who want to be a Fortune 500 CEO. Some want to be President of the United States. Some want to be in politics but not as high as president. There are some who want to be a Doctor or a lawyer. Some want to be a painter or a fashion designer. When I was a kid, I didn't walk around dreaming to be a sales director for a Fortune 500 company. But since I was not a baseball player, singer or football player it was a pretty good option for me.

I don't think any one job is good or better than the other. I think it depends on the individual and what their purpose in life is. Even though I wasn't in my dream job I had developed a strong passion for what I was doing. Perhaps that's what led to the perfect attendance. I believe your passion should allow you to fulfill your purpose. My Corporate America experience provided that for me. In my first book Healthy Marriages, I define my purpose in life.

"In my life, I've always been able to take challenging situations and turn them around. When someone feels he or she is losing the battle of understanding, I can transform it into a positive situation.

I worked in corporate America for nearly 30 years. There I realized I had a pure calling to coach and mentor. I realized I am here to make life better for someone. I am here to help someone understand how to "get it done." I am here to help someone win. I used to think I was called to be a preacher or some great educator, or perhaps a high-level coach because these are innate abilities I possess. But my true calling is walking with people like me, muddling through situation after situation. I want to help each person who wants help. I want to uncover each challenge they face. And in the process of discovery, learn about myself and our common humanity. Then I want to come up with practical and logical ways to overcome the universal struggles we encounter."

I've always loved hearing the story Jessie Owens would tell of the 1936 Olympics when he was about to win his fourth gold medal in the long jump. He was nervously awaiting his turn and even fouled on his first two jumps. The massive crowd was cheering against him and he could feel the eyes of Hitler staring down on him to fail so their own German long jumper could win. To everyone's surprise, and especially to Jessie's, before he would make his final attempt to jump, the German long jumper came over to him, put his hands on his shoulders and began to encourage him. The German jumper gave him advice that would assure he not foul on his final jump. Jessie went on to make the final jump, setting a new world record and obtaining his fourth gold medal of the games. My purpose in life is similar to the German jumper. My purpose is to help people. I go into coaching mode whenever I see anyone in need. I even love helping my daughter with her math homework. I am the absolute worst at math but simply because I know how to help her understand the concepts as I couldn't when I was her age, I've enjoyed helping her pass and get good grades in her math class.

I also believe part of my purpose is sharing the gospel. Not as a preacher but just sharing. In the Bible Matthew chapter 28:19-20 what's referred to as The Great Commission, Jesus says to his disciples "Go ye therefore, and teach all nations... Teaching them to observe all things whatsoever I have commanded you." Of course HE's referring to spreading the gospel. I believe that too is part of my purpose. I think of the countless kids I've coached in football, basketball and baseball and how I broke the game down to them where they could understand and develop into a great player. Many times I've taught them how to see the game from the field or the basketball court and I myself have never even experienced that. The passion is in the desire to help them as I've always wished someone would have helped me. In 1993 my Pop Warner football team won a national championship. I coached my sons' 5th and 6th grade basketball teams to a remarkable two time conference winner in back to back years. Many of those dudes still say those years were their best basketball years in life.

Once while in college I served as a New Student Orientation leader. I was there to help new students get through orientation week. I recall during the registration process there was a White dude who was $5 short. Not paying the $5 would have cost him time and probably a day of getting fully registered. I don't even recall what the $5 was for but I knew I had $5 in my pocket. Before he stepped out of the line I said to him, "No, you've got to stay in line. You don't wanna lose your place." He replied, "But I don't have the $5 they're asking for and my parents have already left." I reached into my pocket and gave him a $5 bill. The only money I had at that time. He said "thank you," stayed in line and completed his registration. Four years later, I was a 5th year graduating senior and he saw me in the student center and said, "You're OJ aren't you?" I said, "Yeah, hey man." He said, "You may not recall but when I was a freshman you gave me $5 to complete my registration and I just want you to know how much I appreciated that act of kindness. You didn't have to do that." I said, "No worries." He then repaid me the $5 I had given him. It made me feel good that someone appreciated my helping them.

I recall once having vanity plates on my truck, which read JLMTIK. Countless times, I'd get asked by people I knew, and even strangers, what does that stand for?

I'd explain JESUS LOVES ME THIS I KNOW. It would always bring a smile and sometimes deeper conversation. My current plates read OJCSU. As people stare they try to figure what college did I attend. Once someone said to me, "I thought you attended Kent State." I said, "I did." They then asked, "Then why is your license plate say CSU?" I explained, "It means ONLY JESUS CAN SAVE US."

This may be simple and corny but I personally feel my purpose is to creatively find ways to share a good word with every one all the time or at least as much as I can. That's why my years in Corporate America were fruitful. I know without a doubt I helped a lot of people excel. Blacks and Whites, men and women, young and old. Some stayed with the company and others moved onto different companies. Some I helped by hiring them and they took off from there. Others I helped by promoting them and that showed them the confidence I had in them. Some I selected to be on my team and that showed them how much I believed in them. Some I showed how to handle a difficult customer in a tough situation and they appreciated seeing me lead by example.

I wrote my second book, my autobiography in an effort to help and inspire people from unfortunate backgrounds realize they can achieve the American dream.

One of the best compliments I ever received in Corporate America was during a sales meeting. One of the SVP's said something like "Everyone who's career has been impacted by OJ in any way please stand." More than half of the group of 100 plus stood up. Some were even people in positions above me. I shall never forget that.

Anyone who's ever worked for me will likely say I was more for helping people than any other manager they've ever had. I believe the sole reason I've coached the years I have is due to the lack of coaching I'd received growing up. I really believe if someone had taken the time with me (as I do with all my kids) I could've been a good baseball player or better football player.

In my Healthy Marriages book, I write I don't believe in a perfect marriage. That would imply perfection. Nothing is ever wrong or will ever go wrong. I don't believe that. Even with couples who have been married 75 years. Bumps in the road build character and helps you grow stronger together. I do believe in healthy relationships and that's what I strive for. I've been married 33 years. I can say we've run into some hurdles and have managed to clear them together and it has enhanced our relationship.

Similarly, I believe the same with the jobs. There is no perfect job. Even the dream job of a Major League Baseball player. They have good and bad days. A postal worker can have a good and a bad day. A doctor can have a good and a bad day yet she loves what she does and is in her dream job. Whether she has friends on the job doesn't define her passion fulfilling her purpose. The main point I'm trying to make is know your purpose. Let your satisfaction come from fulfilling your purpose. You may be on a job and not be appreciated for what you do but if you're fulfilling your purpose, it's all good.

Finally, in my Healthy Marriages book in chapter 19, I write about starting with the end in mind. I speak about the three questions. I feel these three questions are applicable to you and your boss. You can initiate it. You can be the one that adds this into your performance discussion. Companies, if the manager demonstrates a high level of Personal Leadership they may initiate this conversation. I write, "Begin with the three questions that are given next. Even though there's only three, make no mistake they are not quick and easy. They won't improve your relationship in a matter of minutes. Just like a marriage an effective working relationship the with boss and subordinate is a commitment.

So, start at the end with these three questions and discussion.

What do you think of me?

What do I think you think of me?

What do I want you to think of me?

If things are going well in your relationship, you and your spouse may come up with the same answers. But I'm willing to say that nine times out of ten, you won't. That's okay because the idea behind this exercise is to get you moving. If your spouse thinks something you don't like, then view it like an arrow saying, ‹Start here.' What you don't like can begin an ongoing dialogue with your spouse. You may not be in sync. Or you may know each other better than you think. The third possibility is that you both have the same answers, but there are different reasons behind them." Answering these questions with each other can promote exciting discoveries. Remember, the key is that both sides answer and are honest. You should know what your boss thinks of you and your performance. If you think your boss sees you and your performance different from what they actually see, there's an opportunity for alignment. Leaving this conversation your boss should be crystal clear of how you want to be seen. With this comes areas for you to sharpen in an effort to consistently show what needs to be shown. Look at question two - What do I think you think of me? Very self-explanatory but remember, it's extremely important to be honest. There will be no resolution without honesty from both sides.

In high school and in college, psychology was one of my favorite classes. Let's look at **Maslow's hierarchy of needs.** This is a theory in psychology proposed by Abraham Maslow in his 1943 paper, "A Theory of Human Motivation." There is little scientific basis to the theory: Maslow himself noted this criticism. Maslow subsequently extended the idea to include his observations of humans' innate curiosity. His theories parallel many other theories of human developmental psychology, some of which focus on describing the stages of growth in humans. He then created a classification system, which reflected the universal needs of society as its base and then proceeding to more acquired emotions. Maslow's hierarchy of needs is used to study how humans intrinsically partake in behavioral motivation. Maslow used the terms "physiological," "safety," "belonging and love," "social needs" or "esteem," and "self-actualization" to describe the pattern through which human motivations generally move. This means that in order for motivation to arise at the next stage, each stage must be satisfied within the individuals themselves. Additionally, this theory is fundamental in knowing how effort and motivation are correlated when discussing human behavior. Each of these individual levels contain a certain amount of internal sensation that must be met in order for an individual to complete their hierarchy. The goal in Maslow's theory is to attain the fifth level or stage: self-actualization.

The hierarchy remains a very popular framework in sociology research, management training and psychology instruction. Maslow's classification hierarchy has been revised over time. The original hierarchy states that a lower level must be completely satisfied and fulfilled before moving onto a higher pursuit. However, today scholars prefer to think of these levels as continuously overlapping each other. This means that the lower levels may take precedence back over the other levels at any point in time.

Simply, I believe,

Within **THE BASIC NEEDS** are physiological needs (food, water, warmth, rest) and safety needs (security and safety). These in my opinion are the main reasons we work - to provide these to our families. We go to work expecting the safety and security needs also be met. Even the brave who serve in the military. As they fight, they're fighting for our security and safety and ultimately theirs too. As I wrote earlier describing the jobs whenever we work, we provide a talent, skill and/or service in return for pay. Usually, the first thing we do with that pay is cover our BASIC NEEDS.

Within **THE PSYCHOLOGICAL NEEDS** include belonging and love needs; meaning intimate relationships and friendships. Here's where I suggest we don't look for these needs within the workplace. Often people do and sometimes when having these needs not met at work it causes them to leave or have an unpleasant work experience. In my opinion when these needs are met outside of the workplace it can be an indicator of a healthy work life balance. At the same time, if these needs are met at work it makes the workplace that much more special. I recall when I first started with Hershey I attended a sales conference at 18 months in. There I met another dude I connected with and we have remained close friends to this day.

Also, within the psychological needs are Esteem needs. This includes prestige and the feeling of accomplishment. We like to feel good about ourselves and we like it when others feel as good or perhaps even better of ourselves. Have you ever felt at home your family doesn't appreciate you as much as you're appreciated at work? Or the reverse?

It's no crime that these needs are met in the workplace, however, I suggest the destination point to meeting these needs should be outside of the workplace. Simply, because you're not looking for the job to make you whole. You are presenting yourself to the company as a whole which now allows you to be the "best you" as you present yourself at work. A tough boss or a cranky day at work is not going to define who you are because your psychological needs are met elsewhere. At home, at the gym, at church, with family and friends.

Within the **SELF FULFILLMENT NEEDS** you have self-actualization. That is achieving your full potential. That includes creative activities. This is that person who's always on top of their game. The good or bad day at work doesn't define them. They are usually a contributor to the good day at work. Likewise, the good or bad day at home doesn't define them as such. They are the ones that help make the situations at home more pleasant. This person appears to be untouchable because they are not relying on others to make for a good moment for them. This is the person that usually makes those around them better. This person is pretty confident because the other levels have been met and are not relying on each other. In other words, to the person who needs work to meet all of the needs, if that person has a bad day at work their self-fulfilling needs crumble and when that crumbles their psychological needs come crashing down mainly in the area of esteem. When that crumbles they may not be productive as they once were, then they're struggling at work, which now could have a devastating effect on their basic needs. When your basic needs are in jeopardy, some people will "lose it." This is just my opinion.

CHAPTER 12

ACKNOWLEDGING

Acknowledge means to admit to be real or true. To recognize the reality, the existence, the truth or fact. I've titled this chapter because I think it's extremely important to acknowledge what things can and will happen while being Black in Corporate America. We're often surprised when we realize we've been passed over. Or when we see younger and less experienced workers get the promotion over us. I believe it's imperative that we come to realize these things are gonna happen. Unless you're with an elite company who visibly values diversity and inclusion. Those companies do exist but if you've found yourself experiencing any of the situations I've described in this book, you're probably not with that company.

I also believe you can experience this stuff and still climb up the corporate ladder. I think of Clint, Skip, myself and even the divisional president dude. I'm sure there are many others who have. The common denominator is we've all come to acknowledge, pick up the pieces and move on. That is we didn't sit in disbelief, shock and the inability to continually move forward. Perhaps our routes and paths are longer but getting there is more important than getting there first.

During my years with Hershey I was promoted eight to nine times. That's pretty good. Each of those times I always felt it could have been sooner but getting there was the ultimate goal. You might think only eight to nine? Especially, when I know of others who have been promoted more frequently and others who have been promoted less frequently. I imagine there are some who have never experienced a Corporate America job promotion. During my earlier years with the company you were "tapped on the shoulder" when it was time for you to be promoted. I kind of liked that because you'd only be "tapped" when they felt you were ready. Even if you saw others getting "tapped" before you it was all beyond your control. All I could focus on was continually doing the best job. Adding value and learning while growing. That, I could control. I know of several people who have said when they were promoted their position was replaced with two people. I called that "wearing the golden handcuffs." Handcuffed into their position but because they did so much and was so valued the handcuffs were golden. Unfortunately, this may have been a reason their promotions were delayed or never happened.

Clint is an area manager with his company. He has district managers reporting to him. Each district manager has four supervisors reporting to them. Each supervisor has approximately ten sales representatives. Clint has a pretty large team. In his company they were really pushing for tenured managers to be promoted to make space in those roles for new managers. Clint was willing to be promoted or even take a lateral move into another role. He was exemplifying being a team player. Clint is the only African American area manager of the company's 20. There was a newly created role - Area manager of US urban markets. Who better than Clint to step into this role since he is the only African American? He felt he could add a lot of value to this new role which focus was the development of urban markets across the US. Clint applied for what would have been a lateral move for him. He interviewed and did not get the job. That wasn't the worst part. He was notified during a national meeting; during a breakfast meeting with his direct supervisor, a SVP and a member of HR. I will spare you the details but Clint recalls this being the worse day of his career. It's the way he was told he didn't win the job. Each of the three had nothing but negative feedback for him. He recalled hearing such things like "how embarrassing… yours was the worst interview of the process… what did you do to prepare? You could have knocked me over with a feather… I couldn't believe you'd do that bad… and we thought you were this great interview person." Clint recalls he was so stunned that all he could have managed to say was "all you had to do was tell me I didn't get it. Not a one of you had anything positive to say." Then he asked to be excused. He went to his room to try and keep his composure before attending the main session of the national meeting. Skip and I reminded Clint, you've always got to acknowledge this can and will happen with us. I'm sure you weren't as bad as they described because they never gave you any specific constructive feedback. They never shared what the winner offered that you didn't. Sometimes they just want to break you down. Clint replied, "They did just that too." We all laughed and moved on. To make matters even worse, Clint learned the dude they selected was already on performance probation and within two weeks into that new role violated his probation, which lead to his immediate termination. Clint thought "Wow, they were willing to take a chance there versus taking a chance with me who's still here and never been a performance issue." Then we all really laughed at the situation.

Skip recalled a conversation with his SVP supervisor during a performance evaluation. It had been a good year for Skip so it was a good performance conversation. During the conversation his supervisor said, "You know our VP of Customer Industry Affairs just announced he's retiring at the end of the year, you'd be perfect for that role. Is that something you'd be interested in doing? You are the best people person I've seen in awhile. You know everyone, everyone loves you and your social skills are extraordinary. You are one of the most respected people in the industry." Skip thought this was the best compliment he's ever received. Skip thought to himself "Wow! You're asking me this when all I've ever shared was this is what I want? I write this into my performance assessment each year and you're asking me if this is what I want?" He responded, "Absolutely I'd be interested, that's a dream role for me and I know I can do it and represent the company well." The next thing Skip knew, he was at a meeting and on the stage the retiring VP of Industry Affairs announced his replacement would be such n so. One of Skip's peers. One who Skip helped develop a relationship with some of his key customers. One on whom Skip had more than seven years experience over. It had even been publicly announced that no one was faster than Skip when it came to put in an honest days work. Acknowledge brothers. We must acknowledge these kinds of things will happen. We've got to pick ourselves up and keep moving on.

Why would that SVP say that to Skip and never ever follow up with why he didn't get the position? It's as if that conversation never ever happened.

I'm not the type nor have I ever been the type to complain "the White man is holding me down." But I have come to realize that some will if you let them. Some will get in the way of my growth and development. The late Dr. Martin Luther King, Jr., once said, "A man can't ride your back unless it's bent." These are things we must come to acknowledge and move on versus stopping stunned, dazed, amazed and confused. We've got to keep moving forward.

We must also acknowledge and realize that

More is Equal. When we're in the workforce there maybe several times we come to realize we have to do more. Produce more. Get more results just to be equal to our White co-workers. Companies, here's where you can really differentiate your company from others. This is the most obvious thing to see happening. This can easily be stopped. This is another example of what many Blacks will call two sets of rules.

Another area we must always acknowledge is that of being Adaptable.

That is maintaining effectiveness in various environments and with different tasks, different responsibilities and different people. In my opinion

Being Black in Corporate America we already come in demonstrating high levels in this area simply because in many instances our backgrounds are extremely different. I recall once early in my career I was a sales representative working with my boss' boss. He said, "Hey I gotta use a phone." Obviously this was before the birth of cell phones. This was when pay phone booths could be found everywhere. We were within the inner city of Dayton, OH and I stopped at the next phone booth. He panicked and said something like, "whoa whoa whoa don't stop here, don't stop here. I'm sure there's another phone in a better area." I said, "I thought you said you needed a phone right away." He said, "I can wait. I also need to be safe while making my call."

I share this story because many times we as African Americans are told we're not adaptable. I think we are more adaptable than anyone can ever imagine. I could stop in any area and use the phone. That manager could only stop in a predominantly White area to use the phone. Many times we disregard our cultural origins to fit into Corporate America. How often has that been done with Whites?

I recall once during a performance review my manager said something like you're not ready to be promoted yet. The area you need to work on is adaptability. The minute she said that I wanted to take her to that same pay phone to see if she would use it.

We must always, always, always demonstrate very strong and good

Work Ethics. Think back to the chapter on those dimensional behaviors we should show proficient. Think back to the Hank Aaron and Magic Johnson scenarios. No one will ever say they didn't work hard. No one will ever say they lacked time in preparing to be their best. I've always believed having a strong work ethic is allowing my work to demonstrate my belief of my moral benefit to the company and the importance of the work I do would allow me the ability to strengthen my character. You want to be known for what you produce so you work hard at it. I believe whenever we're hired this is an area companies are really quick to look for. I've know of situations where the person could not demonstrate this within their 90 day probationary period and for that reason were released. I believe this can be shown on day one. You don't have to know all the intricacies of the job but you can show that with what you do know, you're a hard worker. I think back to my early days with Hershey. I came out the gates working hard because that was the first thing I wanted them to notice about me. Having good work ethic is what makes you a first round pick on a basketball team.

Another area we must always acknowledge is the fact that our visibility will keep everyone at ease. This prevents the thought of us doing anything negative. This portion is to remind us that BEING SEEN is not always a bad thing. I think of the big meetings whether it's a national or divisional type of meeting. After dinner there's often a dine around. Companies like to see you mixing and mingling with the crowd. Networking with other team members. What they don't want to see is minorities fleeing the scene. Then they start imagining we're up to no good or being anti-social. Being seen just means hang out, play the game. This is another demonstration of our adaptability. Being visible shows your level of social engagement and your willingness to fit in and perhaps be of influence. During my years as a director I'd usually score well in this area. I'd be seen working the crowds. I could walk into any group and socialize with them for a while then head off to the next group. It didn't matter what area of the country they were a part of. I purposely didn't allow myself to go unseen or just be around one person. We have to remember there's probably not many of us in the group. We'll be easily missed.

There is a cause to being seen and that is you don't want to over do it. Let's stick with the same scenario. After dinner there's a dine around. In corporate America that usually means a lot of alcohol. DANGER! DANGER! DANGER! After awhile you start to see people consume beyond their levels of control. This is what I call

Leave the Party Early and be seen leaving. Alone. I've seen too many people commit "corporate suicide." Skip recalls once at a national meeting he was leaving the party early. He had made himself visible and was heading to his room. On the way through the hotel lobby he saw two managers male and female and they were cuddling. Skip knew they were both married and not to each other. He knew the guy very well and didn't know her too well so Skip called him over and asked, "What are you doing?" He then said, "What if you're seen? There's a host of senior leaders about to come through this lounge. This is not a good look." All the guy said was "thanks for the heads up." He then ushered her to his room. They both had way too much to drink. Skip visibly went to his room. Within weeks as a result of that encounter both managers were terminated.

It's important to not get caught up in the after party stuff. You have to recall you're at this meeting not for the purpose of getting free unlimited drinks, and meeting girls or guys. You don't have to be the last one to leave the party. Leaving the party early allows you to be publicly seen by your subordinates, peers and even supervisors leaving without getting into any unprofessional situations. If they leave and you're still there, they may just assume you're doing the wrong things and may show up to work the next day late or hung over or worse not at all.

Remember to always put yourself in a position of both being a Role Model and Mentoring someone. By leaving the party early someone is always watching you. They may have witnessed how you conducted yourself at the meeting, at dinner and during the dine around. They surely noticed you weren't over-consuming alcohol at the drink bar. They noticed when the party started getting wild, you were nowhere to be found. They notice how engaging you are whenever you're in the meetings and even during meals. They are very quick to notice how you carry yourself around people above you and your peers. They can see if you're respected by your peers as knowledgeable and of good judgement and decisiveness. They may have even once overheard their boss speaking high of you and as they observe you they're now witnessing what they've heard. They may be watching you because you're in a position they're aspiring to be in. They may be watching you perhaps because you carry yourself in such a way that their manager suggest they look at someone who does this well.

They may never ever say anything to you. You may never know just how you're inspiring them. Always, always, remember to be a role model even when you're not expecting to be.

Similarly, you should always be looking to supportively mentor someone. Look for that someone who is aspiring to climb the corporate ladder. They could be a subordinate or even a peer. They may ask you something that allows you to share your moral personal perspectives. They will never ever ask you point blank, "Will you be my mentor?" But they may constantly ask you for your thoughts, advice or your perspectives. They may keep in touch with you sharing what their career aspirations are. They may share with you some of their struggles on the job because they think you don't have the same struggles. Or they think whenever you've had the struggles you must have effective figured out how to overcome them. Or they may simply think the struggles you've had are much greater than the struggles they have. Surely, you can help them deal with their struggles.

You shouldn't be surprised even if someone above you admires how you carry yourself. A boss or supervisor may be as bold to let you know they admire your level of professionalism. They may even share your character as a best demonstrated practice while in a public meeting so others know to observe you. All of the above mentioned scenarios have happened with me. Whether subordinate, peer or even supervisor they made sure they let me know somehow. I recall thinking to myself that's great because that is the way I would want to be perceived. Remember the three questions?

What do you think of me?

What do I think you think of me? and

What do I want you to think of me?

In each of the above scenarios they were thinking of me just as I wanted them to think of me and when they mentioned it to me that changed how I assumed they thought of me. You see, I wasn't thinking I was being viewed. I wasn't thinking there was a Senior Leader that admired how I carried myself. I wasn't thinking there was a peer that wanted to score better in their performance evaluation in this area and chose me to share my insights. The main point here is you never know when, and to what extent you're being watched. Make no mistake, being Black in Corporate America you're always being watched.

I believe you always need to show some level of

Intelligence With an Intellectual Approach. What I mean here is simply this. It's unfortunate but we (African Americans) are sometimes perceived as not as intellectual. Not as intelligent as others. You may come to work for a manager that thinks to some degree Blacks are inferior. They may have hired you just to "check a box." You can't control that but you can control how you present yourself. Intelligence means the capacity for learning, reasoning, understanding and similar forms of mental activity. It is a manifestation of a high mental capacity. Meaning "you can grasp the concepts." Intelligence is a constant display of your knowledge and understanding. That being said you want to subconsciously show your employer that "you get it." They don't have to "spoon feed" you. It's ok to ask validating questions to confirm you're on the right track in your thinking. You don't want to be that person that's always the last one to figure it out.

Skip was once in a managers meeting and they were discussing a strategy. The boss said something like "We're going to change our approach. Instead of our usual direct approach we're going to start doing it this way." Because the new approach was so drastically different it puzzled everyone. Whispers and murmuring began as people were trying to understand why and how could this be done. Skip got it. Skip even shared to the group his insight and big picture vision. This was huge because he did it in such a way his peers began to understand. Skip had explained and rationalized the new direction even better than his boss. His boss began reiterating comments Skip had made. The group instantly began to embrace this new direction. This was also a big win because Skip's boss quickly realized he had been bailed out by one of his subordinates. Not in a negative way, but in a supportive and intelligent way.

Intellectual means appealing or engaging the intellect. Guided or developed by relying on the intellect rather than the emotions or feelings. This is what Skip provided to that conversation on that day. As I said during the introduction of this book, Skip is as sharp as they come. Extremely smart and he "gets it." He knows how to adaptively and intellectually play to various people.

Finally, when it comes to acknowledgements I believe it is imperative that we are able to differentiate Calmness vs Passion vs Aggressive vs Assertiveness.

As African Americans we are constantly mislabeled as being overly aggressive. When we show passion it's sometimes perceived as hostile and aggressive. When we try to be more passive we're often labeled as too calm and not passionate. When we try to show our tenacity for getting the job done it's sometimes mistaken for militant aggressive behavior. Calmness defined is without rough emotion - still or nearly still. Free from excitement or passion. Passion defined is a powerful or compelling emotion or feeling; a strong amorous feeling. Here's where we want to be, but for us, unfortunately, they see us as being aggressive. Aggressive defined is unprovoked offensive attacks, invasions or the like. Militantly forward. Making an all out effort to win or succeed. Competitive. We're certainly not that in the workplace. Assertiveness is defined as confidently aggressive or self-assured. Positive. Having a distinctive or pronounced taste or aroma. The only problem with these four words is that for African Americans, three of the four will make some people feel we're hostile and militant. This is why I feel we always need to be aware just to know how we might be perceived. Skip recalled once at a meeting he gathered with friends after dinner just talking, laughing and enjoying each other's company. There were about 10 to 12 people. Skip was one of three African Americans. The other two were at levels below him but they were not members of his team. Assertively, he stood and said, "Well, I'm about to turn in." They had been there for nearly an hour. When he said that the other two African Americans said they were turning in also. A higher ranking VP said, "Wait a minute, what's going on? Are you all about to go do something?" Skip said, "No, I'm turning in." He went left and the other two went in a totally different direction. That was the end of that night. The next day Skip was approached by that VP and asked, "What did y'all get into after you left last night?" He said, "Nothing, I turned in as I'm sure the other two did as well." Then the VP said something like, "It's just the way you said it seemed like it was a calling to gather afterwards." Skip thought to himself, "All I said was I'm turning in." The point here is we can sometimes say things and it's just perceived as something negative. Skip was then told, "Next time let them stay if they want. That was a good networking opportunity for them." He thought to himself, "Wow, now the perception is I'm controlling when people come and go. I must be a Jedi."

Well, if you've made it this far into the book you've experienced a lot of stories. I make no apologies for them because they've all helped build my professional character.

I'm no Bible scholar but I do read it and have a basic understanding. I personally accept the Bible as GOD's inspiring words to me. Perhaps one of my favorite scriptures is Colossians 1:16,17, "All things were created by HIM and for HIM. HE is before all things, and in HIM all things hold together." This helps me because it constantly reminds me that no matter what the situation or circumstance it's a creation by GOD. As I made the decisions I've made within Corporate America. GOD was with me. As I encountered all the situations within my nearly 30 years, GOD created all things. All the people that have come into my path in life, whether in Corporate America or not, GOD is before all things. This is a constant reminder that in GOD all things hold together.

I write this book not with anything but good intentions. I feel if anyone can learn anything from my experiences then it was well worth the write. If any company can learn anything it's worth the write. Many of the situations I write about made me stop and ask myself "what could have prevented that from happening?" None of these occurrences made me drop everything and quit but I imagine there are people who'll say, "It ain't worth it and then look for employment elsewhere."

CONCLUSION

I'd like to think this book touches a lot of nerves. I'm sure there are some who will not enjoy this read for whatever their reasons may be. I respect that. On the other hand, I'm sure there will be many who can relate to the content. Everything within has actually happened. Believe it or not. Fortunate or unfortunate. Good or bad. Sometimes the truth hurts but if it's the truth and we have to deal with it. My mother used to say a tree grows from its roots to be as tall as the sky. It grows many branches. Each branch can grow in different forms, shapes and sizes but they all have come from the same root that produces the same tree trunk. No matter how different the branches have grown they're all still a part of that tree. She'd go on and say the root represents we're all GOD's creation. We've all come from GOD. The tree trunk is GOD's word and Church designed to keep us all connected but sometimes here's where we can begin to differ.

Some branches grow upward. Some grow straight out from the trunk. Some branches grow out then point downward. Some branches have leaves. Some branches have leaves and stems and begin to grow other branches. But still they all come from the same root. GOD. They still have the same trunk. God's word and church. I realize during the Black Lives Matter movement we all witnessed a lot of hostile mobs protesting and tearing down confederate statues. I'm not for that. In fact, I believe as painful as they are those various statues represent a part of history. What I am impressed with is when the city or town decides they no longer want that statue representing them. To me, that's a form of self-conviction. I'd rather have that than a bunch of angry protestors tearing it down.

Whether you are a company seeking to better understand how to connect with minorities in your workplace or if you're actually Black in Corporate America I'd like for you to at least get these seven takeaways from this book.

1) Self-Conviction

When you self-convict, the first thing you want to do is stand in front of the mirror. It is almost impossible to lie to yourself when you look at your reflection. So when you're identifying where you have missed the mark in any of the principles, be sure you are looking at yourself in a mirror. In more contemporary terms, you messed up and you're acknowledging to yourself. I can't emphasize enough how much easier life is when you admit mistakes. The longer you blame someone, or something else, the longer a problematic situation will persist. So, "own up."

2) Capable - KDM shot calling

Perhaps the most important part of the Main Ingredient is when a company has that main KDM (Key Decision Maker) that exercises his/her authority and makes the big call. Many times I've seen situations where there's that one person in a company who could (like Thanos, from the Avengers Infinity War) snap one finger and make things right. I believe every company has this person and can't stress how important it is to connect with this person, if at all possible.

3) The 8 IF's. I believe this alone would solve everything.

Let's look at it on a broader scale. Let's look at all employees. Blacks, Whites, Asians, Hispanic, Indian, men, women, young or old.

If the following were evidently equal for everyone the problem would be solved.

IF they were paid well for what they do.

IF they had an effective mentor within the company helping them with their career path.

IF they found their job or responsibility challenging.

IF they felt they were fairly and timely promoted.

IF they constantly felt they were involved in key decision-making.

IF they were evidently and constantly reminded that they were appreciated and valued.

IF they were empowered to make decisions to help the company win.

IF they were sincerely trusted to do their job.

Companies, IF you can deliver on those "ifs" consistently with EVERY employee I'm willing to bet you'd have a top place of employment not only for African Americans but for every employee. The key is, you can't deliver on the Ifs for some employees and not everyone.

4) I feel these three questions are applicable with you and your boss. You can initiate it. You can be the one that adds this into your performance discussion. Companies, if the manager demonstrates a high level of Personal Leadership they may initiate this conversation.

So, start at the end with these three questions and discussion.

What do you think of me?

What do I think you think of me?

What do I want you to think of me?

Remember, the key is that both side's answer and are honest. You should know what your boss thinks of you and your performance. If you think your boss sees you and your performance different from what they actually see, there's an opportunity for alignment. Leaving this conversation your boss should be crystal clear of how you want to be seen. With this comes areas for you to sharpen in an effort to consistently show what needs to be shown. Look at question two, What do I think you think of me? Very self-explanatory but remember, it's extremely important to be honest. There will be no resolution without honesty from both sides.

5) **The Dimensions of Success**

The first is a triad of dimensional behaviors that I'm calling the 3 I's. Initiative, Impact and Integrity.

The dimensional behavior **INITIATIVE**. Let's define this as being proactive. Making the active efforts to influence events to achieve a positive goal. Being a self-starter versus having to be told or directed all the times. This is the person that often goes above and beyond what is required.

The next is **IMPACT**. Quite simply, making your presence known and remembered. This is the person who "lights up the room" when they enter. All of a sudden all eyes are upon you. This person can create a good impression without even saying a word. They command attention. This can be demonstrated in what you wear and what you say and even how you say it.

The next area is **INTEGRITY**. This is always going to be a must. People must sense you are honest to your word and that you're trustworthy and believable.

The next behavior is **PERSONAL LEADERSHIP**. This is slightly similar but different from initiative. This is the person who on their own does what it takes to make him/herself better. Personal leadership has you setting and achieving the realistic goals you've set for yourself.

Another area is to become proficient in establishing your

INDEPENDENCE; The state of being independent. The freedom from necessary control or influence, support or aid. The company knows you will deliver and they don't have to hold your hand.

The next area I would look for the employee to be strong and proficient in is that of

INTERDEPENDENCE; the quality or condition of being <u>interdependent</u>, or mutually reliant on each other. Capable of being depended on; worthy of trust; reliably strong. They know they can count on you.

BEING BLACK IN CORPORATE AMERICA

It is always imperative to have a **STRONG DRIVE FOR RESULTS.** This is the person that literally gets the job done. This person delivers consistently, time and time again. You almost become more known for this.

6) I think the fastest thing for African Americans in the workplace to easily detect is when there's **two sets of rules.**

Of all the Blacks I've spoken with who work within Corporate America this is the main issue. It often appears what works for others doesn't always work for us. What others get away with we get heavily penalized. What others get approved for we get denied and rejected.

7) **Chapter 13 ACKNOWLEDGING.**

Acknowledge means to admit to be real or true. To recognize the reality, the existence, the truth or fact. I've titled this chapter because I think it's extremely important to acknowledge what things can and will happen while being Black in Corporate America.

Bonus) Communication - Remember the ABCnD's. Becoming **A B**etter **C**ommunicator in **D**ialogue

If you don't want to go through this alone, I make myself available to dive into any or all of this stuff. Companies, I want to help. Employees, I want to help.

Follow me on Facebook @ Ojbtalkin or OJ Smith

visit my website ojbetalkin.com.

Email me @ ojbtalkin@yahoo.com

I'm here to help.

Wow! Wait a minute. Wow! As I'm finishing this book, this just came in. Another shooting of a Black man. Video released of Wisconsin police shooting a Black man multiple times in the back. Police shot Jacob Blake, who witnesses say had been trying to break up an argument between two women, as he walked back toward his silver SUV on Sunday, August 23, 2020. As three of Blake's sons looked on from the rear seat of the vehicle, the officer fired seven times toward Blake's back at close range. I am strongly praying for this situation. This is so current we don't have a lot of details. Even at this point I ask, why not tase him in the back? Was seven shots in the back necessary? Why not prevent him from getting to the car? Make no mistake, I support law enforcement but Wow! Wow! Wow! Here we go again. The NBA, WNBA and some MLB teams have already boycotted games in an effort to call for justice. Corporate America I'm sure this is being discussed in your workplaces.